SLUM *to* CEO *Mindset*

Building Empires from Nothing:
The Slum to CEO Mindset Unveiled

MAHEK SOLANKI

BlueRose ONE.com
Stories Matter
NewDelhi • London

BLUEROSE PUBLISHERS
India | U.K.

BlueRoseONE.com
Stories Matter
NewDelhi • London

For permissions requests or inquiries regarding this publication, please contact:

BLUEROSE PUBLISHERS
www.BlueRoseONE.com
info@bluerosepublishers.com
+91 8882 898 898
+4407342408967

ISBN: 978-93-5989-854-4

Cover design: Shivam
Typesetting: Namrata Saini

First Edition: March 2024

Contents

Introduction

Have you ever wondered what it takes to transform a poor mindset into a CEO mindset? To go from a life of struggle and limitations to one of success and abundance? Well, my dear reader, buckle up because you are about to embark on a journey that will not only blow your mind but also inspire you to unlock your true potential.

Welcome to my world, where dreams become reality and where the power of mindset reigns supreme. In this book, titled "Slum to CEO mindset ", I will take you on a BRTS bus ride through the various stages of my life, sharing with you the trials, tribulations, and triumphs that have shaped me into the

Sharing the hardships, sufferings, and successes that have turned me into the person I am today with you.

Let me paint you a picture: imagine a young, wide-eyed youngster growing up in the center of a bustling city. This young man, whom we'll name Mahek Solanki, comes from a low-income family where every cent counts and aspirations are considered a luxury. But Mahek had no idea that his lowly origins were the seeds of an astonishing change.

As you delve into the pages of this book, you will walk through the dusty streets of my childhood, where friendships were forged and dreams were kindled amidst the chaos of everyday life. You will see the difficulties encountered by a little youngster with a terrible attitude who is surrounded by unpleasant circumstances. But, dear reader, prepare to be amazed, for this is not a story of despair, but rather a tale of unwavering determination and resilience.

The journey continues as we enter the realm of teenagehood, where school becomes a battleground and societal expectations threaten to suffocate the dreams within. In those formative years, I felt the weight of the world on my shoulders, but I refused to let the circumstances define me. I sought out knowledge, devoured books, and absorbed every piece of wisdom I could find, all in the pursuit of personal growth. With an inexhaustible appetite for information, I began my professional career, joining the corporate world with wide-eyed optimism and a quest for achievement. It was here that I first met the reality of the working world, including harsh competition and apparently insurmountable challenges. Rather of succumbing to the demands, I saw them as possibilities for progress.

Through the pages of this book, you will witness my ascent from one job to another, each step bringing me closer to my ultimate goal of becoming a CEO of my own life. I will share with you the lessons I learned along the way, the mistakes I made, and the victories I celebrated. But above all, I will implore you to persevere, to never give up on your dreams, no matter how daunting the journey may seem.

But this is not just a story of personal triumph; it is also a tale of societal change. In the chapters that follow, you will bear witness to the power of equality, as I showcase how women can shatter glass ceilings and rewrite the narrative of success. I will shine a light on the extraordinary power of motherhood, revealing how a mother's love and sacrifice can propel her child to greatness.

Finally, this book is an homage to dads, those hidden warriors whose efforts are sometimes overlooked. I will take you on a heartfelt journey through the sacrifices my father made, the challenges he overcame, and the unwavering support he provided as I embarked on the path to success.

So, my dear reader, are you ready to join me on this extraordinary journey? Prepare to be captivated, to be inspired, and to embrace your inner CEO mindset. Together, we will defy the odds, break barriers, and create a world where dreams become reality.

Welcome to a story of transformation, confusion, resilience, and limitless potential. Welcome to "Slum to CEO mindset" by Mahek Solanki.

CHAPTER 1

From Poverty to Ambition

The Influence of Childhood

We had a wonderful childhood when we played street games; 1990's kid upbringing was filled with amazing video games, cartoons, and television shows that today's generation may not have. I was born in the early 2000s, not the 1990s, but I know that complete childhood is the time where our mind set begins to build our personality and we begin to build the stage where we believe whatever we are told by our elders. Every incident, good or bad, affects us, and our decisions are based on emotions. Poor people believe that this is their destiny, whereas rich people believe that they can create their own destiny. I discovered this through observation, and my father taught me to analyze everything. He taught me chess when I was five years old, and he knows how my mindset will develop, and my mother believes that I will break this chain and put myself first.

Understanding Slums

A slum is an overcrowded urban residential area with inadequate infrastructure and poor living conditions. These areas arise due to various factors: rapid rural-to-urban migration, economic stagnation, poverty, informal economies, inadequate planning, political issues, natural disasters, and social conflicts

Residents in slums face significant challenges such as unsafe living conditions, overcrowding, limited access, or the absence of essential services like water, sanitation, electricity, and transportation. Their homes are often unstable and vulnerable to damage from storms or earthquakes. Moreover, there's a lack of secure land tenure or property rights.

The prevalence of slums is a global issue, affecting millions, particularly in developing nations. Projections indicate that by 2030, one in four people worldwide will live in a slum.

Efforts to tackle this problem include various strategies such as slum removal, relocation, upgrading, urban planning, and the implementation of public housing projects.

Sociology of Slums: Examining Urban Human Settlements Post-Liberalization

The post-liberalization era has witnessed significant shifts in the ecological landscape. Urbanization has soared, with half of the global population now residing in cities and towns. This transition has also brought forth the emergence of deprived urban settlements. These settlements, home to a substantial portion of cities like Mumbai, Nairobi, and Mexico City, exhibit glaring inequality through poverty prevalent within slums.

Slums serve as concrete evidence of intra-city inequality and widespread urban poverty, perpetuating social exploitation and denying inhabitants their basic human rights. Sociology studies how slums impact social structures, community dynamics, and disorganization, shedding light on aspects like social cohesion, human resources, and ecological elements within a societal context. While not all slum residents live in uniform poverty, it's crucial to acknowledge that slums generally fall below acceptable living and working conditions.

The generalization that states that all people who live in the slums are poor is false, but it should be noted that the slums, in general, have below-minimum living and working conditions.

Slum Characteristics

Slums are a crucial and ongoing concern in urban contexts, sometimes viewed as hotbeds of crime and health risks. Sociologists have conducted significant research in these districts, which stretch from Bangkok to London and are distinguished by poorly constructed houses nestled in packed, narrow alleyways with high humidity and exposed drainage systems.

Even affluent nations like America have a considerable portion of their urban population residing in substandard housing. Socialist nations, despite extensive urban renewal programs and limitations on private land ownership, also contend with slum areas. According to the UN Habitat, slums are defined as areas where individuals reside under the same roof, lacking one or more of the following: permanent housing safeguarding against adverse weather conditions, adequate living space for multiple inhabitants, and easy access to safe water. (UN-Habitat, 2007)

Debates persist regarding the role of slums in shaping identities and vice versa, contributing to ongoing discussions.

Ghetto vs. Slum: Understanding the Differences

A ghetto and a slum, although both describing impoverished areas within a city, carry distinct meanings and origins.

Ghetto Definition and Origin:

- A ghetto is an area where an ethnic, racial, religious, or cultural group is isolated or segregated from the larger metropolitan landscape. Segregation is frequently caused by discriminatory behaviors, oppression, or past brutality. The term "ghetto" originates from the Italian word for "foundry," referencing the region in Venice where Jews were forcibly relocated during the 16th century.

Key Differences:

Definition Basis:

- A ghetto's defining characteristic lies in the composition of its residents, emphasizing the identity of the inhabitants. In contrast, a slum's definition revolves around the quality and condition of the area itself.
- Formation Causes:

Ghettos often emerge due to external forces or policies that deliberately separate or marginalize a specific group. Conversely, slums tend to develop internally, influenced by factors like rapid urbanization, poverty, or insufficient governance.

- Community and Identity:

Ghettos may foster a stronger sense of community and cultural identity among residents who share common backgrounds and historical experiences.

- Overlap and coexistence:

While a ghetto and a slum have distinct characteristics, they often overlap or coexist. Not every ghetto is necessarily a slum, and not every slum qualifies as a ghetto.

The distinctions between ghettos and slums underscore the varied origins and defining factors shaping these marginalized urban areas.

I hope this helps you understand the difference between a ghetto and a slum.

Some examples of ghettos are:

- The Venetian Ghetto
- The Nazi ghettos in Europe,
- The Shanghai Ghetto in China
- The African American ghettos
- Chinatowns, which are ethnic enclaves in numerous places across the world where Chinese immigrants and their descendants reside and retain their culture and identity, were established as ghettos as a result of anti-Chinese legislation and practices, while others were established willingly or for economic reasons. Chinatown in San Francisco, Chinatown in London, and Chinatown in Bangkok are a few instances.

I hope you understand some differences between slum and ghetto, but I do not 100% belong to slum and also not 100% belong to ghetto culture, but there is one concept: there are small towns.

Slums, ghettos, and tiny towns are all terms used to represent distinct sorts of human settlements that may have some degree of poor overcrowding, but they also have diverse meanings and origins.

1. A small town is a human settlement that is larger than a village but smaller than a city and usually has some degree of local government and economic activity.
2. Some of the common challenges faced by slums, ghettos, and small towns are:

Poverty and inequality: Residents of slums, ghettos, and tiny towns may have poor incomes, restricted opportunities, and limited access to resources and services. In addition, they may experience social marginalization, discrimination, or stigma from the rest of society. Crime and violence: People living in slums, ghettos, and small towns may experience or witness crime and violence, such as theft, robbery, assault, or murder. They may also face threats from gangs, militias, or extremists. They may have little or no protection from the law or the authorities.

Some of the differences in challenges faced by slums, ghettos, and small towns are:

Culture and identity: People living in ghettos may have a stronger sense of community and cultural identity than people living in slums or small towns, as they share a common background and history. They may also have their own language, religion, or customs. However, they may also face more discrimination, oppression, or violence from other groups or the government, especially if there are differences in beliefs, values, or interests.

Development and innovation: Because small towns have more economic activity, infrastructure, and government, they may have greater development and innovation than slums or ghettos. They may have more access to technology, information, and education. However, they may experience increased rivalry, pressure, or change as a result of societal urbanization, globalization, or modernization. Diversity and integration: People living in slums may have more diversity and integration than people living in ghettos or small towns, as they have more migration, mobility, and interaction with different people. They may also have more adaptation, flexibility, and creativity. However, they may also face more conflict, tension, or instability from the rapid and unplanned growth, change, or diversity of the population.

However, they may also face more conflict, tension, or instability from the rapid and unplanned growth, change, or diversity of the population. And within this, one common thing I have observed is the mindset. All people have one mindset, which we can say is a fixed mindset, and this mindset is more dangerous than any situation they are facing.

Breaking Free from Limiting Beliefs.

During my formative years, I received messages indicating that I could not achieve remarkable feats. Although my parents had good intentions, their mindset led them to believe that life would perpetually be a struggle and that success was exclusively reserved for an elite few. But they fought through situations and created a good time for me. Over time, their beliefs seeped into my subconscious, causing me to internalize them.

As I transitioned into adulthood, I found myself burdened with self-doubt and insecurities. I habitually compared myself to others, convinced that they were destined for success while I was, by nature, flawed. Fearing that failure would only validate the beliefs I had been exposed to my entire life—that I was inadequate—I refrained from taking risks and chose caution instead.

However, a voice deep within me insisted on proving the untruth of these ideas. I became determined to prove them incorrect and to break free from the self-imposed constraints I had accepted. In pursuit of advice, I devoured self-help material, listened to motivational lectures, and sought mentoring from outstanding people who had also overcome similar problems. This transforming journey taught me the importance of changing one's mentality and growing self-assurance in order to overcome constraining ideas. I realized that success was not a gift but rather the result of hard work, unrelenting determination, and, most importantly, a good attitude.

I gradually embraced the notion that I, too, had the potential to achieve excellence and construct the life of my dreams. One of the most impactful transformative shifts in my mindset was the re-evaluation of failure. Rather than viewing it as confirmation of my deficiencies, I began to perceive it as an avenue for personal growth and education. I grasped that failure should not be regarded as an endpoint but rather as a stepping stone on the path to success. This cognitive shift empowered me to take greater risks and embrace the unknown, understanding that even in the face of failure, invaluable lessons could be gleaned.

Another vital aspect of shedding limiting beliefs entailed surrounding myself with a supportive and encouraging network. I recognized the influential role my circle of acquaintances played in molding my mindset and shaping my perception of myself and my abilities. Consequently, I distanced myself from negative influences and actively sought out like-minded individuals who valued my potential and fostered my aspirations.

I eventually realized the benefits of my efforts through the passage of time, constant work, and an unyielding conviction in my talents. With confidence, I took on new projects and routinely pushed myself beyond my comfort zone. I reached previously unthinkable goals, and with each accomplishment, my self-belief became stronger. Breaking free from restrictive ideas did not happen overnight. Rather, it required years of dedication, fortitude, and unwavering faith in my own abilities. Nonetheless, the difficult trek was well worth it. As I reflect on my personal change today, I am glad for the trials that forced me to question my ideas and nurture a different perspective.

Embracing Ambition

Throughout my childhood, I was encouraged to be content with what I had rather than aspire for more. People frequently reminded us that we were regular people destined to live ordinary lives, rendering great goals meaningless. For a long time, I accepted this mental system and resigned myself to a life of ordinary successes, but my father, who never realized these things, brought me anything I asked for, and my mother reared me as if I were a prince. However, when I approached my late twenties, a strong stirring within me grew. I began to doubt the story that had been implanted in me since infancy. Was it genuinely wrong to strive for more? Could genuine happiness be achieved if I settled for a life imbued with complacency? These questions incessantly pestered me, necessitating the discovery of answers tailored to my individual needs.

While browsing the shelves of a neighborhood bookshop one chance day, a book titled "The Power of Ambition" quickly piqued my interest. Its appealing cover and fascinating title encouraged me to give it a try. I had no idea that this book would be the spark for a dramatic paradigm change in my life. As I read through the pages of "The Power of Ambition," I came across stories of regular people who dared to dream and eventually achieved incredible accomplishments. These people endured tremendous challenges and setbacks, yet they adamantly refused to grant their circumstances the power to define them. Instead, they wholeheartedly embraced ambition, employing it as an indomitable force propelling them towards their objectives. Perusing these narratives, I was enlightened to the fact that ambition ought not to be perceived as a source of trepidation or disdain but rather as a tool that can be harnessed to construct an improved existence. This newfound realization demanded a transformation in my mindset. I realized that I had been traversing life in a perpetual state of complacency, abstaining from personal and professional growth or excellence. However, armed with this newfound understanding and perspective, I felt emboldened to embark upon a journey of comprehensive transformation. Embracing ambition signified breaking free from the self-imposed limitations that had impeded my progress. It entailed believing firmly in my capabilities and acknowledging that I possess the agency to shape my destiny. It necessitated challenging the prevailing status quo and daring to dream on a grand scale, even when such aspirations appeared insurmountable.

Nevertheless, embracing ambition was not merely an exercise in dreaminess; it required concerted action. I understood that if I intended to actualize my ambitions, I must devote considerable effort and unwavering dedication. It entailed stepping beyond the boundaries of my comfort zone, confronting my fears head-on, and persisting through adversity, even during the most arduous stretches of this pursuit. Amidst this transformative process, doubt periodically threatened to infiltrate my thoughts. I questioned whether I genuinely possessed the ability to achieve the echelon of success that I ardently desired.

In these moments of uncertainty, however, I reminded myself of the testimonials I had read—stories of ordinary people who performed genuinely extraordinary accomplishments. Furthermore, I surrounded myself with people who shared my ambitious desire and had unflinching trust in my abilities. Their continuous support and encouragement were vital as I faced the obstacles that lay ahead of me. We built a community of dreamers, constantly pushing and inspiring one another to achieve previously unachievable goals.

Reflecting upon my personal journey, I assert with confidence that embracing ambition manifested as the most momentous decision I have made thus far. It enabled me to transcend my circumstances and forge a life that I had once envisioned solely in my dreams. However, more significantly, it unveiled the true power of self-belief and the immense potential that resides within every one of us.

As a result, I advise any striving person who comes across these words to embrace ambition entirely. Hold on to an unrelenting desire for achievement and an unwavering commitment to climb above your circumstances. Believe in your own ability and understand that you have the necessary characteristics to make your ambitions a reality. While the trip may not be simple, it is unquestionably worthwhile. Let us work together to create a society in which ambition is valued, ambitions are compassionately nurtured, and individuals are completely encouraged to attain their full potential. Remember that this transformation starts with a shift in mindset: from complacency to a relentless pursuit of achievement. Accept ambition and go out on the path to your ambitions.

- Belief systems and mindsets intricately shape our perceptions and behaviors, constituting integral aspects of human psychology. They serve as foundational frameworks, woven from our experiences, cultural influences, and societal interactions, which fundamentally impact our understanding of the world.

Beliefs function as cognitive lenses, defining our values, attitudes, and decision-making processes. These mental constructions shape our identities and drive our behaviors, and they are strongly entrenched in personal experiences and communal learning. The interplay between our beliefs and mindsets molds our approaches to challenges, influences how we embrace opportunities, and ultimately shapes the trajectory of our lives.

Furthermore, the psychological phenomenon of confirmation bias frequently strengthens current ideas, leading us to seek evidence that supports our pre-existing opinions. This tendency hardens our opinions, perhaps making it difficult to accept alternate positions.

However, comprehending the psychology behind beliefs empowers us to introspect, evaluate, and potentially reshape our outlooks. It encourages the exploration of diverse viewpoints, nurtures empathy and critical thinking, and fosters a more nuanced understanding of the world around us.

CHAPTER 2

Is it bad to Dream Big?

Some people think that dreaming big is a bad thing. They think that it's unrealistic, impractical, or even harmful. They think that it's better to be realistic, practical, or even humble. But I disagree. I think that dreaming big is a wonderful thing. It's a gift that we all have, and we should cherish it.

Dreaming big allows us to imagine a better future for ourselves and for others. It helps us see the possibilities and opportunities that lie ahead. It helps us set goals and plan actions that can make our dreams come true. It helps us create value and solve problems that matter.

Dreaming big also motivates us to take action and make a difference. It pushes us to work hard, to learn new skills, to overcome challenges, and to achieve results. It pushes us to collaborate with others, to share our ideas, to support our peers, and to inspire our followers.

Dreaming big also challenges us to grow and learn. It makes us face our fears, our doubts, and our limitations. It makes us question our assumptions, our beliefs, and our values. It makes us explore new perspectives, new experiences, and new knowledge.

Dreaming big also enriches our lives and our souls. It fills us with passion, joy, and satisfaction. It fills us with purpose, meaning, and fulfillment. It fills us with happiness, confidence, and gratitude.

In this chapter, I will share with you some of my dreams and how they inspired my life for the better. I will also reveal to you the sources of inspiration that helped me shape and refine my dream vision, and how you can use them to craft your own.

1. Confusion

- Everything was okay until I turned 16. That was the time when I needed to make some decisions on my own. Until then, my parents used to make decisions for me, but now I had to make decisions about my studies and career myself. I found that there was so much confusion inside me.
- What to do?
- Why to do?
- How to do it?
- What is good?
- What is bad?

I didn't even know what I wanted or why I wanted it. I didn't even know what was right for me and what was wrong for me. During college, I found that I am probably an introverted person. I didn't even know properly:

- How do I talk?
- What to say?

And nothing represents the confusion of an introverted person more than when their mothers take them to general stores to buy pulses and rice, and there is confusion as to which pulses the mother had ordered and, if they're not available, which pulses have to be brought. There was bound to be so much confusion because everything I had lived until now, whatever I had aspired for, was fulfilled by my parents. Whatever I wanted due to my stubbornness, my parents also fulfilled it for me. But now, whatever decision I take will be for me, and that is where my future will be. Yet, I never took anything so seriously. When I was 15, I had just given my 10th standard board exam, and it was summer vacation. Most of my friends had started working; some of them had already begun supporting their fathers in work; one had started working as a plumber; one went with his father to a construction site; one started working in a medical store; and one started working in a mobile shop. And there was me, still playing with street children. I found a sudden change a year ago; the friends who were excited to go on vacation to play games, enjoy cartoons, and play video games were not available this vacation.

When I asked one of my friends why he was not coming to play nowadays, as it was vacation, he replied that he helped to support his father at work, and anyway, we are not children anymore. Slowly, the circle got smaller and smaller, and now only I and some young children were left.

After some time, one of our neighbors asked me to do some work or support my father. I replied to him, "It's vacation, so what? You are not a child anymore," and I went back home. My parents were discussing something about me, and when I asked what happened, my mother told me, "Why don't you support your father at work? After all, you are free nowadays."

I got angry that night, but after a few days, I decided to work at a medical agency as a delivery boy. It was my first job, and I was doing it at 15. Soon, I will be turning 16 in June. With the help of my friend's request, I started working at the medical agency. I remember my salary being decided at Rs.2,000 per month. I was happy because, at that time, 2K was also a big amount for me, and I could buy a smartphone for myself at that time.

It was a 9:00 a.m. to 8:00 p.m. job; at first, it started with basic inventory work to understand which medicine was where. After 10 days, I started delivering medicine to different medical stores in Una by bicycle because I didn't have a vehicle license.

Now, reality was coming to my eyes. I took a bag full of medicine with my ID card and supplied medicine to various places, sometimes clinics, pharmacies, and sometimes hospitals. From 10:00 a.m. to 4:00 p.m., I was doing the same. Slowly, I got tired, both physically and mentally. In between, I texted weekly, and for the first time, I realized that it could be a career.

One day, I went to a clinic to deliver medicine; the doctor asked me if I was studying. I replied, "I recently gave my 10th exam, sir. Here is your bill." The doctor observed that I could read English and the names of medicines, so when I was about to leave the clinic to deliver to others, he suggested, "Child, make sure you complete your education." For the first time, I took something seriously because, until that day, I had never focused much on studying. Teachers had advised me to focus on education, but I realized that day.

It was summer, and the temperature was high. After collecting all the bills for the month, I left that job.

After that job, I realized that there were many people who were doing this kind of hard work very early. When it was time to select a stream, I was willing to join the science stream, but I opted for commerce. I got news that when school started, almost all my friends got separated due to some reasons; some of them failed, and others abandoned their studies. Some then went abroad to study. I continued studying.

- At that time, I didn't know how to overcome confusion, but here are some points that can help you do so:
- Priority and organization: arrange tasks in order of importance for clarity.

- Seek Clarification: ask questions to gain a clearer understanding swiftly.
- Break Down Complexity: divide complex problems into manageable parts.
- Seek support and guidance; consult mentors or experts for advice.
- Mindfulness and Reflection: Take breaks to reflect and regain focus.
- Develop clear strategies: establish clear plans and steps to follow.
- But every choice I have made in my life has been majorly taken in confusion until I decided why.

2. Confusion in Finding the Why Behind Dreams
3. After completing high school, I chose to take admission in management studies. I opted for a BBA (Bachelor of Business Administration).

Starting college, I chose management studies to avoid math, believing it wouldn't be part of the program. But to my surprise, I ended up with advanced math courses. I was puzzled, wondering how this happened.

The reason was that I was not clear about my why and reason, while my other friends who had cleared high school were researching and finding universities for better careers, and some of them were planning to go abroad.

I picked management studies to avoid numbers, but here I was, facing them. At first, I was disappointed and confused. However, I started to wonder: could these math classes actually help me understand business better? Maybe numbers weren't that scary after all.

It was June 8th, my first day of college. I turned 18 that day and stepped into college. I thought things would magically sort themselves out because I was now an official adult, but that's not how it turned out. The confusion I expected to clear only got worse.

Being an adult wasn't as simple as I thought. It wasn't just about turning a certain age; it was about facing a bunch of real-world problems I hadn't imagined.

My idea of being an adult fell apart as I realized there was a lot more to it than I ever thought. It was like a wake-up call to me—the fact that life isn't as straightforward as I had hoped. Suddenly, I found myself dealing with tricky situations I had never learned about in school. The confusion wasn't just about turning 18; it was the start of a journey into life's complicated twists and turns.

I became an adult, but my inner child was still there. My college professor once asked me, "What is life going to be?" This was a common question asked by teachers during school, but this time it hit differently.

Everyone who was there had a reason, but some of them did not have a clear reason and probably did not have a proper plan. I was one of them, and a similar reason I observed among them was money.

It all starts with the primary need: money.

When the professor asked me, my answer was, "A satisfied, happy, and healthy life." But it all started with the primary need: money. So, what can money fulfill after primary needs?

- Hobbies

- Life style
- Will (Appentence)
- Dream

And the last thing is goals, which include this in one

Like I said before, life goals always remind us that human needs are infinite.

'Goals are so-term or long-term reasons, which we said with the plan'

So there are many types of goals.

- Life goal
- Family goal
- Social goal
- Economic goal (primary)

However, health is connected with personal goals.

Happiness is for me connected with family and friends.

Satisfaction is connected with karma; it is connected with society as well as personal goals, and the third primary need is money, which is connected with the economic goal. If I combine these four, it will be a life goal.

My professor understands why finding the goal of life is important.

I asked the professor, "How can I find my 'why'?" I am still not clear with my 'why'.

He replied, "Ask yourself. You can find your way by asking yourself only or by finding out what your dream was when you were in school. Find out something that inspired you more, or who your role model is, or what is the thing that you like the most."

I started thinking about it. One day, as usual, I went to college by bicycle. I observed that the parking area was full of bikes, board bikes, and cars. Only one bicycle was there, which was mine. I felt different. These changes are usually felt.

With the passing time, I felt I was not getting connected that much with people. I can clearly feel the environmental changes that make college different from school. After some time, I found I have one personality trait called introversion.

I found that I am hesitant to talk with people. My behavior is getting strange with people. And that was the age. I started to observe myself and those around me.

Luckily, I made three friends in college, but I realized that when I was in school, I had 50 people in groups who were my friends. Walt has already been introduced to the internet, but 2016 and 17 were revolutionary years. Because of India, we forced them to get free internet, and I bought my first Ford mobile with the help of pocket money.

So with the help of free internet, people will now get more engaged with each other after radio, television, computers, and mobile phones.

Now it was time for a smartphone wait and high-speed internet.

Now curiosity was increasing in me, but with that, I was going to develop multiple personalities for myself. I didn't know.

It was Sunday when I went to support my father at work. I saw he was already reading a book. I asked my father, "You are reading a book, and with that, you are selling fields as well. How do you manage both? And why are you still reading books?"

He replied, "Learning is a continuous process, and you can learn from books, whatever you want. Remember, learning is a continuous process that continues through life."

I replied to my father, "When I was in school, one of the school teachers used to tell us that books are human best friends, but whenever I read, I can't focus more and get sleepy."

Father replied, "It is because you read books to finish school, syllabus, or college tests and exams. Try some authors' books and some writers' books. It could be any of your interests."

Imagine being lost in a maze of expectations, where everyone hands you a piece of a puzzle, claiming it's your 'why.' That's how it felt—this quest for my 'why.' It was like sorting through a pile of mismatched socks, trying to find the perfect pair.

Everywhere I turned, someone said, "Follow your passion!" But what if my passion wasn't a straight road but a winding river with too many forks? The pressure to pick a single 'why' made my head spin.

Then came the chorus of advice: "Do what pays well!" or "Do what makes you happy!" Conflicting voices turned my head into a carousel, leaving me dizzy and unsure.

It was a constant tug-of-war between what I loved, what others expected, and what seemed practical. I was stuck in a mental traffic jam, unsure which lane to take.

The struggle was real—peeling off layers of 'shoulds,' 'musts,' and 'have-tos' to find the real me underneath. It was like trying to read a map in a storm, seeking clarity amidst chaos.

But slowly, like gathering scattered puzzle pieces, I began piecing together my interests, dreams, and values. The path to my 'why' started clearing, revealing a direction that felt authentically mine.

So to understand the 'why' of life and seek answers to life's puzzles as I navigate this labyrinth, I tried many things. Here are five points that I started in order to clarify my 'why'.

Exploring Freely:

I tried various things, just like tasting different flavors. Figuring out what excited me and what didn't was my way forward.

Listening Carefully:

I paid heed to advice as if I were choosing my favorite song. I kept what felt right to me, disregarding what didn't resonate.

Dreaming Fearlessly:

I imagined my future without any boundaries, much like drawing with no rules. Dreams, I realized, could evolve and expand.

Reflecting Inwardly:

Taking quiet moments to ponder what truly mattered to me felt like gazing at my favorite picture, seeking answers within.

Embrace the Uniqueness: Collect rare puzzle pieces, each representing a unique trait, to create a mosaic that celebrates your authentic self.

Thinking big was just the start; now comes the 'how.'

I tried different things—sports, YouTube, art—to figure out what clicked.

Along the way, I discovered more about people and how our minds work, especially through studying psychology and management studies.

The next part isn't just dreaming; it's doing.

It's about trying stuff out and understanding the real deal behind our dreams. Each try teaches something new about me and the world.

Join me on this journey of figuring out what makes us tick..tick.

CHAPTER 3

From Rookie to Rockstar

The comfort zone is a state of mind where you feel comfortable, safe, and at ease. It is where you rely on your intuition, faith, and connection to guide you. It is where you experience happiness, dreams, confidence, self-esteem, health, and passion. But the comfort zone is also a trap. It can limit your growth, potential, and creativity. It can prevent you from achieving success, excitement, love, expression, fun, abundance, fulfillment, and joy.

To break free from the comfort zone, you need to:

- Challenge yourself.
- Take risks.
- Explore new possibilities.

You need to embrace:

- Uncertainty
- Discomfort
- Failure

You need to:

- Stretch your boundaries.
- Expand your horizons.
- Discover your true self.

Only then can you unleash your full potential and live your best life.

I read it somewhere in a book.

I learned about the comfort zone, a state of mind where I felt comfortable, safe, and at ease. I discovered the benefits and drawbacks of staying in my comfort zone and how it affected my happiness, success (I've not succeeded yet), and fulfillment. I also learned how to break free from my comfort zone by challenging myself, taking risks, and exploring new possibilities. I found practical tips and exercises to help me stretch my boundaries, expand my horizons, and discover my true self.

When I know about the matrix concept in my personal life, It is a metaphor for the illusion of reality that we create in our minds based on our beliefs, perceptions, and expectations. It is also a way of describing the system of control and manipulation that society imposes on us through the media, education, religion, politics, etc.

I started some research and started learning about the history of various geographical areas and their cultures.

The matrix is not something that we can escape from once and for all. It is something that we have to constantly be aware of and question. It is something that we have to choose to transcend every day by making conscious decisions that align with our values, goals, and purpose. It is something that we have to create for ourselves by using our imagination, creativity, and willpower.

When it comes to history, most people ignore it, but history has the answer to your question today. The whole history of any country taught or learned in one hour of a school period is difficult. So, if we want a solution to today's problem, we will have to know the history, but always remember that in every book, the history writer has written with his own intention and understanding. You do not have to believe without arguments; you just have to know, and this is also possible. The secret of any future problem should be in our present today; today is our future, and tomorrow is our today.

So, in this excitement, I started following whatever was easily available to me in my matrix. In this process, I joined the Communist Party. With time, I realized that the questions I had were actually related to the Communist Party of this group. But they were not doing anything special to solve the problem. They were just blaming the government. I also did the same thing for a few months, and then I started questioning whether the government would do its work by itself, but am I working for myself? Am I not a responsible person? I have to work hard for my dreams; will the government come and fulfill them? No. And I understood from the matrix that in reality, my thoughts are not mine; they have come from somewhere under the influence of or inspired by someone's words, which means that in my time someone is using my time for their politics, and that is fine, but I was not getting any benefit from it, and that is not fine.

That's why if you do not start working on your dream, someone else will hire you to fulfill theirs.

Then I started learning from available sources and focused on developing my skills first. I left that Communist Party, but from there, I first found that politics is quite an interesting subject; directly or indirectly, we are all connected to it.

The forgotten culture

There are many cultures that we don't know much about. They were hidden in the past. They are the remains of amazing people who lived long ago and had their own ways of life and beliefs that made them human. Many things can make these cultures disappear. Wars, attacks, disasters, or changes in society can all make them go away. And these cultures have a lot to teach us. They are like parts of a big puzzle that we need to solve. They show us how different people lived and thought in different times and places. Every thing they left behind, every old piece of writing they made, helps us connect with them and learn from them. They remind us of where we came from and what it means to be human.

The culture of India is also vast and deep. Every part of India has its own faith, culture, and customs, but my question was whether every culture really takes 100 years to arise and end. The answer is no.

This happens every ten years as technology and inventions enter our lifestyle. This system will also keep changing, but are people making changes in their lives accordingly? The technology that was invented for the use of humans today, with the help of psychology, is using humans instead, which no one is even aware of. And even if they are aware, it has become their habit. If they come out of one matrix, they will get stuck in another. The level of marketing today is such that there is no privacy even in the data that is being used for it. And if we look at the history of the last 30 years, what were villages yesterday are small cities today, and small cities today will be mega cities tomorrow. So those who upgrade themselves with every small change maintain their existence for a long time. Where an important role is played by education, and I observe that people are depending on the government, Educating yourself is important. In India, there was a Gurukul culture for education. Now a day has disappeared. But knowledge is everywhere; just take a book of new skills or knowledge you want to learn.

So I understand my town's past history and its culture, and I get an idea of how economics and politics affect most people.

The middle class illusion: is being average enough?

If we go through the income-based approach, which divides the population into different income categories based on their annual household income, there are four main classes: the poor, middle class, low-income, high-income, and the rich. Different countries and regions may have different definitions and criteria for classifying social groups.

I have heard some biases about the poor and middle class. The idea that trying to be middle-class or poor is actually a bad thing because it means you are stuck in struggle is real, and you don't aim for better things. But is it true?

Some people say that the middle-class trap is a problem for many countries, especially developing countries. Some biases about it are:

The middle-class trap is a personal problem that affects people who are afraid to take risks, try new things, or challenge themselves.

They say that these people are comfortable with their current situation, but they are not happy or fulfilled.

They say that these people need to change their mindset, habits, and choices and aim for higher goals and bigger dreams.

But is it true?

I don't know, but when I heard that, curiosity got boosted in me. And I read some books, watched some lectures and videos, and found some common tips:

Invest in your education and skills, and keep learning new things.

Save mentors and role models who can inspire and guide you.

Surround yourself with positive and supportive people who share your vision.

Take action and pursue your passions, and don't let others stop you.

But one important factor in all these is learning about financial literacy, in which I am very bad. I am still learning this. It is an important skill that can help us achieve our financial goals and avoid common pitfalls.

You can create a realistic budget and track your spending.

You can pay off your debt and improve your credit score.

You can save, invest your money wisely, and grow your wealth.

You can plan for your retirement and secure your future.

You can protect yourself and your family from financial risks and scams.

There are many ways to improve our financial literacy, like reading books and magazines that cover various financial topics, listening to podcasts that offer practical tips, taking online courses, etc.

It's okay to be average. If someone has grown up in an environment where hard work and physical pain are common, then if you try to explain to that person the value of a peaceful environment, chances are that he may find it boring. But in the future, his generation will not tolerate that hard and risky work. If he wants to practice something else instead of choosing it, then he will have to fight with that belief and environment, which means he will have to fight with himself also. So a belief is formed that living in big houses is not within our control; in fact, one does not even know whether the house is small or big. It depends only on the values of life. The difficulty lies only in the arrangement. In a big house, the arrangement is favorable for him; in a small house, the arrangement is favorable for the small one.

It is all about management, isn't it? I don't know, but this is one of the reasons I chose the management stream.

My Career Ladder: The Diary of Career Exploration

When we enter college, we usually start thinking about our career, right? Some smart people may have already planned their future while they were in school, but I was not one of them. I had no idea what I wanted to do or why. So, as usual, I took advice from people around me. One common thing that came to everyone's mind was how I could earn more money in a short time. That's what I started thinking about while I was in college. When I was in school, I had a different vision. I wanted to help the poor and do something useful for society. But then I realized that the poor child who needed help was me. So, when I asked for suggestions from people, some of the common things I heard from them were: start preparing for UPSC and GPSC exams; join the police or army training; or get a job somewhere to learn something first. These were some of the options I had to choose from.

I will share with you what I have tried to do to choose my career path and the vision behind every action. I have failed many times, but I have also learned a lot from my experiences. I started writing a journal when I turned 18, and I want to take you through my daily diary entries, where I have recorded some of my career stories.

YouTube:

One day, I went to Tapovan, a place where I often visit. There is a temple of Shree Hanuman and a river called Marchhundari near the temple. When my friends and I were coming back from there, we saw a person playing a flute on the roadside. He was also selling flutes. I love music, so I wanted to buy a flute from him. But I didn't have enough money. My friend Harshit helped me with ten rupees, and I had forty rupees. The flute cost fifty rupees. I bought the flute and tried to play it. Somehow, I managed to make some sound. After one month, I could play some tunes with it. My neighbor friend Ashok heard me and asked me, "Why don't you make a channel on YouTube?" I was shocked and said, "Channel?" He said, "Yes, where you can upload your videos and earn some money."

It was 2018, and 4G internet was connecting people easily. I had seen some YouTubers who had channels since 2015 or earlier. So, when my friend Ashok suggested that we start a YouTube channel, I agreed. I didn't have a smartphone, but Ashok did, so we created a channel on his phone. Ashok didn't know English very well, but I did, so whenever we had a problem, I emailed YouTube support when it needed it and kept updated on the new policies. Ashok helped me with editing and shooting videos. But when we started making videos of flute playing, we faced challenges. The first challenge was that I didn't know music, so I could only make some unclear tunes. I needed to learn the flute from an expert, but that would take time and money. We didn't have enough budget, so we changed the name of our channel and started making videos of Gujarati song remixes using some online software. Our videos started getting more views, and after three months, we got our first payment from YouTube. But unfortunately, YouTube changed their policies, and the next month, we got copyright strikes and lost our channel. Then we created another channel where we uploaded other people's videos, but we failed again. Then we made another channel of gaming videos because action games were very popular at the time and YouTube had a new live feature for gamers. But we still had limited resources and not enough vision, and we failed again.

GPSC, UPSC, and government job preparation:

It was January 2019, and I was working at my father's handcart. I realized that I was not good at bargaining, and I felt uncomfortable in this place. I had to be focused and careful so that no one would steal or eat the fruits. The good thing about living in a small town or village is that everyone knows you and is connected with you. In the evening, I went to the playground, where I had completed my 11th and 12th studies. I love sports, so I was running there. I saw a lot of people on the ground, and I asked my friend Pradeep, "Why are there so many people today?" He said, "Army vacancies are coming, and they are preparing for them. You are 18 now; why don't you try? You are good at running; you just need to boost your stamina and complete the ground running in a few minutes." I said, "If it's possible, let's give it a try." I started preparing for the army by running, jumping, and studying. But later, I found out that I needed to weigh at least 50 kg, and I was only 46 kg. So I gave up after preparing for three months. One day, I went to the barber shop to cut my hair, and he suggested that I prepare for GPSC and UPSC exams for government jobs. He told me how people respect civil servants and how government jobs have security and help in getting married easily.

I started preparing for these competitive exams along with my college studies, but I found it hard to focus on both. I needed to learn time management, so I allocated one hour for this preparation at night. It was self-preparation, because joining any classes or academy was beyond my budget. After some time, my enthusiasm went down when I heard news about how some people cheated on the exams and how the results got delayed or cancelled. I saw that out of 2000 vacancies, 5 lakh people applied. I calculated the competition and realized that academic scores mattered a lot. I had very low scores. I saw how people from lower backgrounds cracked these exams and became successful. Then I convinced myself that I have to serve the country, and that can be done by doing some other work too. After a year, I give up.

Hostel life:

During the Diwali vacation, my college friend Ravji told me about a training program that he had recently joined. It was a course on logistics management, where we could learn about logistics and supply chain management. The course was offered by National Skills India, a government initiative. In November 2019, I went to the Amreli Center, where they had hostel facilities for the students. They offered various types of courses, and I chose the warehouse management and packaging course. At that time, I was thinking about quitting college and starting a job to earn money. But my manager and center coach, Desur Bhammar, sir, advised me to complete my studies first. It was the first time I experienced hostel life. After completing the course, I got an internship project from my college.

I chose to do it at Sheetal Ice Cream, an ice cream manufacturing company in Ameli.

During the Diwali vacation, my college friend Ravji told me about a training program that he had recently joined. It was a course on logistics management, where we could learn about logistics and supply chain management. The course was offered by National Skills India, a government initiative. In November 2019, I went to the Amreli Center, where they had hostel facilities for the students. They offered various types of courses, and I chose the warehouse management and packaging course. At that time, I was thinking about quitting college and starting a job to earn money. But my manager and center coach, Deshur Bhammar, sir, advised me to complete my studies first. It was the first time I experienced hostel life. After completing the course, I got an internship project from my college.

I chose to do it at Sheetal Ice Cream, an ice cream manufacturing company in Amreli. There, I learned about the operation and packaging of the product and marketing strategies.There, I learned about the operation and packaging of the product and marketing strategies.

Living in a hostel teaches you self-management because you have to take care of everything by yourself. When I was entering the last year of college, I was planning to start a job for experience at Adani Ports or somewhere else where I could learn and develop my career. I also wanted to study for an MBA after that, but my financial situation was not allowing me to do so. But then, in 2020, the world pandemic COVID-19 arrived in India. On March 25, 2020, the Indian government announced a lockdown.

At that time, I had just come back from the hostel to my home because I was not feeling well. This lockdown changed my life in many ways.

COVID-19 and lockdown:

COVID-19 is a disease caused by a new strain of coronavirus that was first detected in China in late 2019 and has since spread to almost every country in the world, causing a global health emergency and a severe economic downturn. The symptoms of COVID-19 can range from mild to severe, and some people may have no symptoms at all. The most common symptoms are fever, cough, shortness of breath, and loss of taste or smell. The disease can be transmitted through respiratory droplets, contact with infected surfaces, or close contact with infected people. The best ways to prevent COVID-19 are to wear a mask, maintain physical distance, wash hands frequently, and avoid crowded places. There are several vaccines that have been developed and approved for COVID-19, but their availability and distribution vary by country and region.

Lock down

Lockdown is a measure taken by governments to restrict the movement and activities of people in order to contain the spread of COVID-19. Lockdowns can vary in their duration, intensity, and scope, depending on the situation and the objectives of the authorities.

Lockdowns can have significant effects on the personal financial situation of individuals and households, as well as on the world economy. Some of the effects include loss of income, reduced consumption, increased debt, unemployment, poverty, inequality, and social unrest. Lockdowns can also affect the mental and physical health of people, as well as their education, social relationships, and access to essential services.

Work-from-home culture and financial impact

Work-from-home culture is a way of working that allows employees to perform their tasks and duties from their homes or other locations instead of going to a physical office or workplace. Work-from-home culture has become more prevalent and popular during the COVID-19 pandemic, as many businesses and organizations have adopted it as a way to protect their workers and customers from the virus, as well as to save costs and increase productivity. The work-from-home culture has some advantages and disadvantages for both employers and employees. Some of the advantages are flexibility, convenience, comfort, autonomy, and reduced commuting. Some of the disadvantages are isolation, distraction, communication challenges, lack of supervision, and blurred boundaries between work and personal life.

According to some studies, the COVID-19 pandemic and the lockdowns have had a negative impact on the income, savings, spending, and debt of many people, especially those who work in the informal sector, the service sector, or the gig economy. Many people have lost their jobs, faced reduced hours or wages, or struggled to find new opportunities. Many people have also faced difficulties paying their bills, rent, mortgage, or loans, or accessing financial assistance or relief programs. Some people have also had to dip into their savings, sell their assets, or borrow money to cope with the crisis.

Important of village life

During the COVID-19 pandemic and lockdown, village life has faced many challenges and opportunities. On one hand, village life has been affected by the health risks, economic hardships, and social disruptions caused by the virus and the restrictions. Many villagers have lost their income, livelihoods, and access to essential services. Many villagers have also faced difficulties returning to their homes or migrating to urban areas. On the other hand, village life has also shown resilience, adaptability, and solidarity in coping with the crisis. Many villagers have relied on their local resources, networks, and traditions to sustain themselves and help others. Village life is important for the recovery and transformation of a country after the COVID-19 pandemic and lockdown.

Impact on me

When you have nothing to do, you have a lot to do. That's what happened to me. The first 21 days of lockdown were normal but challenging. Then, when the government announced six months of lockdown, I went through many phases. I couldn't go out of my home, and the television and news were full of COVID-19 content. I stopped watching negative news from outside. Now, let me tell you what side effects I got from lockdown. 1. I started to observe things more. 2. I started to read the study books that I had hardly touched before. After finishing my college books, I asked my high school teachers, Damodar sir and Ram sir, to give me some books for reading. They gave me psychology and Gujarati literature books. 3. I visited my notes board, where I had pasted some sticky notes in 2018. I had written some skills to develop on them, and I started working on them. 4. I focused on self-discipline because I was so messed up with my daily routine. 5. I got addicted to my mobile phone because I used to watch so many movies and web series. I started to limit my use of my mobile phone. 6. I started to learn about human behavior and attitudes. 8. I started practicing yoga and meditation. 8. I started focusing on my strengths and weaknesses and became more self-aware. 9. I started my own thela (handcart) to earn money. 10. I learned how to deal with depression and anxiety. The lockdown affected me in both negative and positive ways. At first, all sources of income were closed, but later, as per the guidelines, we could sell fruits for some hours. I started my own business to support my father. After that, reading books, practicing discipline, yoga, and meditation, becoming more self-aware, measuring my self-development, and managing my mental health were the things I realized during the lockdown.

Another important thing was to complete my studies, which I was about to abandon, but my mother supported me, and somehow I completed them. Most people were getting mass promotions, but I was in the last year, so I had to give exams. Luckily, I had studied those books in lockdown, so I passed with average percentages. I also fell into some scams, like MLM and crypto, in order to earn money from home. I lost some and also gained some relationships. This one year of lockdown felt like many years because I developed so much in it, which I probably hadn't done before. I boosted my confidence level from zero. Now I just want to experience everything, so I planned to move to another city, Ahmedabad, where I was about to develop my actual CEO mindset. In the next chapter, I will tell you how to develop a CEO mindset. I will also tell you how I learned from my hobbies and how you can learn from them too. Spirituality helped me become more self-aware.

CHAPTER 4

Off Comfort Zone: Una to Ahmedabad

Venturing into YouTube and content creation, I recognized the promising career prospects but acknowledged my lack of essential skills for success in these fields. This realization echoed a similar sentiment when I opted out of the GPSC and UPSC exams. The crux lay in understanding that experiential knowledge often outweighs textbook learning.

The disparity between theory and practice became evident, particularly as I observed numerous young individuals pursuing careers without a clear vision or mindset. This trend seemed inefficient, prompting me to foster a curiosity to absorb diverse experiences and knowledge.

Understanding that comfort could yield happiness, dreams, confidence, and self-esteem, I also grasped the importance of challenging myself for personal growth. The decision to step out of my comfort zone materialized when I chose to relocate to a new city, Ahmedabad. My cousin brother, Rahul Solanki, who was diligently working to carve out his career in Ahmedabad, lent his support, promising to assist me in exploring opportunities in the city.

Packing my bag with the financial support of my mother, I embarked on this new journey on October 4th, 2021. The next day, as I arrived in Ahmedabad, I couldn't help but notice the stark changes since my last visit on February 16th, 2016, when I participated in a state chess tournament.

Alighting at Shivranjani Cross Road early in the morning, I reached out to my cousin Rahul, who promptly picked me up and guided me to his place. Ahmedabad, renowned as one of the safest and fastest-growing cities, greeted me with awe-inspiring skyscrapers. The city's people, characterized by their business acumen, sweetness, and supportiveness, left a positive impression. I admired the efficient and convenient BRTS transportation system.

Beyond the urban landscape, Ahmedabad revealed its rich cultural heritage through historical monuments, museums, and festivals. As the largest city in Gujarat, Ahmedabad encapsulates the state's diversity, prosperity, and vibrancy. Gujarat's history, economic strength, and distinctive cuisine unfolded before me, adding depth to my learning experience in Ahmedabad.

Flat no.: M11/116

Upon my relocation to Ahmedabad, I faced the choice of either opting for a PG or sharing a room with my cousins. Due to the ongoing pandemic, some roommates were working from home, making it feasible for me to stay there. Mr. Saurabh, the room manager, graciously allowed me to join. Thus commenced my remarkable journey of stepping out of my comfort zone, with the primary goal of pursuing my MBA studies.

Before delving into my MBA pursuit, let me introduce you to the vibrant individuals who constitute the members of Flat No. M11/116. Although our numbers have fluctuated due to shifting job locations, each member adds a unique flavor to our living arrangement, akin to different flowers in one bouquet.

Firstly, there's Saurabh Bhai, an experienced individual working for a fintech finance company. Having ascended to the role of chief manager, he boasts incredible money management skills. Next is Harit Bhai, an HR recruiter and the man responsible for room management after Saurabh Bhai. Known for his straightforward and direct approach, Harit adds his distinctive touch.

Then comes my cousin Rahul, an accountant with skills surpassing his academic qualifications. Despite being older than me, he's still pursuing further education. Lakhan Bhai, studying chartered accounting, follows. His kind-hearted nature and deep love for cricket are complemented by a touch of "angry young man."

Ashish Rathod, a corporate employee on a break due to marriage, contributes his presence. Amber Bhai, an IT professional and the practical critic of the group, hails from Maharashtra. Bhavik Bhai, the sole entrepreneur in our midst, brings his experience in Dubai hotel management.

The list extends to some ex-roommates, such as Ram Bhai from Bihar, Lalji the engineer, Neel working in US taxation, J.D. Bhai the corporate employee, Vivek involved in RERA and a former CA aspirant, and our newest addition, Rajpal Bhai, a regional collection manager from Punjab.

Last but not least, there's me, Mahek, fondly known as BABA, a nickname bestowed by Saurabh Bhai and Lakhan Bhai. The lessons I've gleaned from my roommates could fill a book.

Each member of our diverse group carries their own unique struggle story, transforming our living space into an adventure. Financial challenges, investment dilemmas, heartbreak, relationship complexities, and academic hurdles—everyone navigates these issues while chasing their dreams. Our room's narrative mirrors the story of every individual who leaves the familiarity of their hometown or village to embrace the responsibilities and dreams that a big city holds.

From Slum to Suit: My First Steps into the Corporate World

Upon my arrival in Ahmedabad, I spent three days acquainting myself with the city. My cousin Rahul, who worked as an accountant, graciously introduced me to the corporate environment by taking me to his office. Entering this realm was challenging due to the scarcity of jobs, a prevailing reality. Nonetheless, armed with willingness and skills, I remained optimistic about securing a position. My first shot at an interview came through a reference from our roommate, Ashish Rathod. Unfortunately, I didn't succeed, experiencing the familiar feelings of anxiety, low confidence, and stress after the encounter. Despite the setback, I considered it a learning experience and moved forward.

Fortuitously, another opportunity arose in the form of an apprenticeship, referred to by Ram Bhai, an ex-roommate. Embracing the chance to gain practical experience, I worked as an apprentice in an MNC company, receiving my initial stipend—a momentous occasion—and my first salary. Overjoyed, I promptly shared the news with my parents. After completing the apprenticeship, I faced the ongoing challenge of managing living costs. During this period, I made friends like Amandeep and Rohit, my first corporate colleagues.

Motivated to explore new opportunities, I applied for another job with Rohit's reference and succeeded in cracking the interview. This marked my entry into the corporate world as an official employee, a significant milestone in my professional journey.

Firsts are profound moments that define our lives, serving as milestones reflecting growth, change, and achievements. Whether it's the initial day of school, a job, or any other inaugural experience, they share a common thread—they signify the beginning of something new. Firsts offer opportunities for self-discovery, challenge, expression, and connection with others. They become cherished memories, stories, and lessons that shape our identity.

Maintaining a habit of journaling, I documented my daily experiences and observations. While securing a job proved challenging, the subsequent struggle to survive and thrive in the corporate world was even more demanding. It was in this process that I grasped the significance of mentors, guidance, and support. As a complete freshman, I faced challenges beyond the theoretical knowledge I acquired in college. Many skills require hands-on experience, emphasizing the value of learning through practical engagement.

This experience unfolded as a comprehensive journey, offering insights into mindset, mentorship, attitude, behavior, self-development, the ebb and flow of life, the importance of healthy habits, and the value of reading books. The corporate world, often defined by rules, laws, goals, and flaws, presented a dynamic landscape with both pros and cons. The story that follows is a testament to the lessons learned and the growth achieved amid the complexities of corporate life.

Mentors and peers

Mentors play a pivotal role in one's corporate journey, providing valuable guidance and insights.

Fortunately, I have been blessed with mentors throughout my life, including school teachers, tuition instructors, and music tutors. In the corporate realm, mentors can emerge from various roles—seniors, team leaders, executives, managers, or colleagues. The learning one derives from them depends on personal initiative. Landing a job in a conducive work culture was a stroke of luck, and my corporate experience echoes similar tales. Let me share mine.

On my first day, a mix of nervousness and anxiety accompanied the trainer's product knowledge session. It was during this time that I encountered my first mentor, Jay Shah. His guidance proved invaluable whenever I needed support, making him a constant pillar of encouragement. Another significant mentor was Sawfan, whose reaction to an accidental tea spill became a lesson in confidence-building. This was also the day we were asked to introduce ourselves, and my nervousness got the better of me, hindering my ability to articulate properly.

Post-training, as I stepped onto the work floor, I found a supportive group of colleagues. Everyone spoke positively about a certain individual, and after seven days, someone, in a scolding tone, asked me, "Where is such a remote?" The intention was to convey a message to a team member without causing offense directly. Recognizing my newness in the organization, this individual, Kandarp sir, approached me later, becoming a mentor and guiding me through my journey.

There was an instance where I got late to the office due to taking the bus. Anand Bhai Panchal, a senior, played the role of a mentor by assisting with transportation. Then, during my interview, Prakash sir and Anand Naidu sir, along with HR Swati, played crucial roles, for which I am grateful. Prakash sir was my team leader, and Naidu sir became my manager, both instrumental in my learning curve.

While our organization had a "no sir or ma'am" policy to emphasize equality, I used these titles to show respect to my mentors. My manager, Anand Naidu, was a significant figure. We attended many meetings together, where he pointed out my mistakes and accepted feedback for improvement. Aasha Ma'am, from another department, provided guidance and used sticky notes for goal-setting, contributing to my growth.

My roommates also played mentorship roles, starting with my cousin Rahul, who was a constant support. Saurabh Bhai, Lakhan Bhai, Bhavik Bhai, and others contributed significantly. The biggest support came from my team: Paresh Bhai, Jhanvi, Anjali, Nikita, Minaxi, Prashant, Akshat, Umang, Shivani, Nirav, Muskan, Anish Bhai, Bhagyashree, and many more whose names I cannot mention individually, but I am profoundly grateful for their mentorship roles in shaping my corporate journey.

Freshers challenges

As a fresher, I faced some challenges that I think every fresher can face. These challenges are not only faced by freshmen but by every new candidate who is going to join a new organization. Here are some of the challenges I faced as a freshman.

Hesitation while sharing opinions: Freshers may lack the confidence and experience to voice their thoughts in front of other staff. They may need to overcome their fear and speak up when necessary.

Adjustment to the new environment: Freshers may find it hard to adapt to the office culture, rules, and protocols. They may feel out of place or awkward at first. They may need to communicate with other people and learn from them.

Time management: Freshmen may struggle to balance their work and personal lives. They may have limited time to complete their tasks and meet their deadlines. They may need to prioritize and plan their work accordingly.

Lack of technological knowledge: Freshmen may not be familiar with the technology or software that their job requires. They may face confusion or difficulties at first. They may need to ask questions and learn quickly.

Working as a team: Freshers may not be comfortable working in a team. They may have different opinions or styles of working. They may need to cooperate and collaborate with others.

Performance and feedback: Freshers may face pressure and expectations to perform well in their job. They may also receive criticism or feedback from their seniors or managers. They may need to accept and improve on their mistakes.

Let me tell you that it's okay if you fail any of them. I have failed many times too, because sometimes we forget that we have a personal life as well as a professional one. Just be self-aware and learn from your mistakes.

One of the biggest problems I had during my professional career was comments from my manager about my actions. It included how I communicated, collaborated, and handled a variety of working situations and interactions. As a self-aware individual, I saw the need to address this difficulty, but my learning technique was different from traditional methods. Faced with this behavioral difficulty on a regular basis, I became curious about how others handled similar situations.

During my investigations, I realized that some people were skilled at concealing their true sentiments and intentions, effectively putting on an act. However, authenticity was a vital value for me, and I was unwilling to compromise it. Nonetheless, realizing the importance of conforming to professional standards, I chose to face this problem head-on.

I chose an alternative path and enrolled in drama classes, namely an acting workshop. Surprisingly, I discovered that a school acquaintance, Dhaval Modasiya, was also attending the same session, and we happened to be coworkers at the same organization. This was the start of my journey to better understand and refine my conduct through the lens of acting.

Upon deeper reflection, I identified that my introverted personality contributed significantly to the behavioral challenges I faced. Seeking solutions, I delved into the literature on personality switching and gained valuable insights during my time at the acting workshop. This multidimensional approach allowed me to amalgamate theoretical knowledge with practical techniques.

A pivotal moment in this transformative journey occurred when I seized an opportunity to play a role in a Gujarati movie as a background artist during a Saturday night shoot. This experience provided firsthand exposure to the intricacies of acting and the demands it imposed. The night shoot concluded with the director calling "pack up," prompting a chaotic dispersal of crew members. This initial foray into acting underscored the inherent difficulties and challenges associated with the craft.

As I continue to grapple with and learn from this behavior challenge, each experience, whether in the acting workshop or on a movie set, adds a layer to my understanding. My commitment to authenticity remains unwavering, but I recognize the importance of navigating the professional landscape with flexibility. The journey to overcome this challenge is ongoing, and with each endeavor, I strive to strike a balance between authenticity and adaptability.

Ups and downs as a corporate employee in India

Being a corporate employee in India or anywhere is not easy. You have to work hard from 9 to 5, or sometimes even longer, to meet the expectations of your employer and clients. You have to deal with the stress, pressure, and competition that come with your job. You have to cope with the changing technology and skills that your job requires.

But your work is not the only thing that matters. You also have to balance your personal life, which is full of responsibilities and obligations. You have to respect and follow Indian culture and traditions, which may sometimes clash with corporate culture. You have to celebrate the festivals and occasions with your family and friends, which may affect your work schedule and productivity. You have to manage your relationships with your society and community, which may have different views and values from yours.

You also have to take care of your finances, which may not be easy. You may not be able to save enough money for your future goals and needs. You may not have enough time and money to enjoy your hobbies and passions. You may not have enough freedom and flexibility to pursue your dreams and aspirations.

These are some of the challenges that corporate employees in India face. They have to juggle multiple roles and expectations and find a way to harmonize them. They have to overcome the difficulties and frustrations and find a way to grow and thrive. They have to make the best of their situation and find a way to be happy and fulfilled.

We are normalizing these things, but what if we don't? What if we try to change, and change happens? COVID-19 and lockdown have taught us many interesting things. I found that the corporate world has a culture that is made by the people, with some rules and regulations. Japan has developed by understanding these things. Every culture should match every country and its people, because we are working for ourselves. And yes, some kind of work is responsible, where we need to sacrifice some important things for national security and other reasons.

Break and Jump

During this period, my grandmother passed away, which was a challenging time for me. However, my team and manager proved to be a strong support system, aiding me through the difficult moments. After attending to family matters in the village, I returned to my routine job. Seeking a change, I embarked on a trip with Harsh Pandya and Sunil, a colleague, to rejuvenate myself. Following this, I made the decision to part ways with the organization, driven by the desire to explore new opportunities that aligned with my skills and aspirations.

Taking a break, I secured another job, this time with a focus on addressing my weakness—communication skills. An excellent opportunity arose in an IT company, and I am grateful to my new team leader, Hett, and HR Khyati for having faith in my potential and hiring me. The organizational culture, being hybrid, was a novel experience for me. However, I had to swiftly turn my weakness into a strength to meet performance expectations and key performance indicators (KPIs).

Time constraints pressed me to prove myself, and my trainer, Divyang, put in significant effort to coach me. Despite the support from HR Omesh, I struggled to meet expectations, impacting the overall team performance. It was during this period of introspection, where I was jotting down my thoughts to understand my shortcomings, that a significant realization dawned upon me. My trainer noticed my proficiency in writing and suggested that I should pursue a career as a writer.

This revelation brought to mind a goal I had set back in 2018—to write a book. Motivated by this rediscovered aspiration, I made the decision to take a break from my current role and focus on fulfilling my long-standing dream. Thus, my journey of leaving my comfort zone continued. Along the way, I engaged in travel, delved into spirituality, developed healthy habits, and garnered invaluable lessons.

In the upcoming chapters, I will delve into the lessons I have learned so far. Additionally, there is another tale, "Broken," which encapsulates yet another short story of leaving one's comfort zone. While it may not be a part of my biography, if the opportunity arises, I will share it briefly.

CHAPTER 5

Leadership Light

What I have learned from challenges and opportunities of the corporate world

Writing this chapter, I recall the many experiences that have influenced my journey.

I've gained valuable insights from the peaks and valleys of my career, reshaping my perspective on leadership. My aim is to share these lessons with fellow young individuals aspiring to make a positive impact in society.

The corporate realm resembles a vast, turbulent ocean, demanding leaders to navigate uncharted territories and confront uncertainties. In this dynamic environment, the qualities of effective leadership emerge as beacons of guidance and inspiration.

Throughout my journey, I've encountered diverse individuals who have deepened my understanding of leadership. From mentors generously sharing wisdom to teammates displaying unwavering loyalty, each person has contributed to the mosaic of my leadership philosophy.

One central challenge in leadership lies in striking the right balance between authority and empathy. How does one motivate and guide a team while remaining attuned to their individual needs and aspirations? This dilemma is at the core of many leadership dilemmas.

To surmount this challenge, I've come to recognize that effective leadership isn't about control; it's about empowerment. By fostering a culture of open communication and mutual respect, leaders can create an environment where every team member feels valued and motivated to deliver their best.

This approach yields profound impacts, as evidenced by the remarkable growth and unity it fosters within teams. By empowering individuals to take ownership of their roles and collaborate seamlessly, leaders ignite a collective synergy, propelling the entire organization toward success.

As I think about these experiences, I am aware of the inherent complexities and nuances of leadership.

It is not a fixed formula but a dynamic combination of adaptability, emotional intelligence, and strategic foresight.

By recognizing these intricacies, leaders can develop a more comprehensive and sustainable way of leading their teams.

Graphical representations and images can also explain the dynamics of effective leadership, showing the interrelated web of relationships and strategies that support successful leadership.

At its core, the essence of effective leadership goes beyond the corporate realm.

Leadership profoundly influences the fabric of society, shaping communities and fostering collective progress. Enhancing our leadership skills extends beyond personal success in our professional pursuits; it becomes a pivotal element in contributing to broader societal advancement. In this exploration of leadership nuances, I encourage reflection on a fundamental question: How can aspiring leaders cultivate a leadership style that not only ensures success within organizational realms but also catalyzes positive societal change? This query acts as a guiding force, propelling us toward a richer comprehension of the transformative potential inherent in effective leadership.

Within this narrative, I endeavor to provide a glimpse into the multifaceted realm of leadership, drawing from my personal experiences. The journey unfolds from a mindset rooted in challenging circumstances to one aligned with the mindset of a CEO. Through these insights, my intention is to ignite a sense of curiosity and introspection. It's a narrative centered on experiential learning, acknowledging that there is still much to be gained on this ongoing journey of growth and development.

Leadership

In the corporate world, a common saying prevails: "Too many chiefs and too few Indians." This phrase implies a desire for leadership roles without a willingness to follow, insinuating that effective leaders are domineering, greedy, and intimidating. However, this perspective is outdated. In India, there is a preference for leaders who embody kindness, care, and generosity rather than those who resort to bullying or rudeness. The evolving information economy demands adaptable leaders, ones who listen, embrace change, and encourage others rather than seeking rigid control.

The central question arises: How can one lead without exerting control? The answer lies in embracing versatility. Leaders should not attempt to cater to every individual's expectations but rather embody adaptability, strength, and flexibility. True leaders influence positive change and empower others without succumbing to burnout. Additionally, effective leadership involves continual learning, fostering improvement, and inspiring others to do the same. This chapter emphasizes the importance of adopting a learner's mindset, facilitating adaptability, collaboration, resilience, and overall enjoyment. Whether in a corporate setting or personal life, the lessons outlined here aim to guide individuals toward becoming versatile leaders who navigate challenges with a learning-oriented approach.

Work harmoniously

Being warm and friendly can open many doors and make you go far. Don't mind the cynics; they don't succeed. Connect with the tough ones by being genuine and sincere. Don't fake your feelings or expect benefits. Those are extras; the main thing is to work harmoniously.

Make your own place

We can be happier and more productive if we look for common ground with others, at home or at work. But we often focus on the differences. How can we find the common factors? For example, at work, you may have a difficult colleague or boss. How can you connect with them? I learned that asking simple questions and showing interest in others can create great conversations. People like to talk about themselves. If the work culture is mistrustful, don't take obvious sides. Be aware of the power dynamics. Build alliances and find common areas for cooperation and understanding. This will help you form strong bonds based on respect and trust.

Office politics and dealing with it

Navigating organizational politics has become an inherent aspect of the contemporary workplace. Individuals respond differently to these dynamics, shaped by their personalities and attitudes. Some adopt an "Ostrich" approach, choosing to ignore the power play around them. In contrast, others embody the traits of an "eagle," remaining aware of the organizational landscape while maintaining a composed and focused demeanor. The most effective strategy for handling organizational politics is to emulate the characteristics of an eagle: an observer, analyzer, and strategic actor. Eagles, being intelligent creatures, can adeptly navigate and, if necessary, respond to the challenges presented.

Encounters with organizational politics may require you to engage in metaphorical battles. Colleagues might engage in spreading unfavorable rumors or attempt to hinder your career progression. In such situations, it becomes imperative to confront these challenges directly and defend your professional standing. Additionally, evaluating the trustworthiness and discretion of those around you becomes crucial. Careful consideration is warranted when sharing personal information or opinions, requiring a balance between being respectful and cordial while maintaining assertiveness and confidence in your dealings.

Being nice

Being busy or frustrated at work is no excuse to hurt others. The corporate world is full of people who ruin their careers by being careless and cruel. If you pursue success at any cost, you may enjoy it briefly, but not for long. You will have many enemies who want to drag you down. I believe that being cordial always wins over being cutthroat. So be cordial; it pays off in the long run. If you respect and value others' work, you will gain their trust and support. Your cordiality will be returned, and you will have an edge when you work with others.

Office meetings and impressions

Before the conference, research the topics and speakers that interest you. Think of some questions that can add value to the discussion or challenge the views of the speakers.

When the session is open for questions, stand up, introduce yourself, thank the speakers, and ask a clear and concise question. Be respectful and avoid criticizing the speakers or their organizations.

Use humor to break the ice and make the speakers feel comfortable. This can also help you get noticed and network with other attendees.

If someone else asks a question before you, you can either build on it or ask a different question that relates to the session. You can also compare or contrast what you heard with other sessions.

Don't talk too much, or try to be another speaker. Keep your questions short and relevant.

If you miss the chance to ask a question, you can approach the speaker later and have a brief conversation. Watch their body language, and be polite. You can also introduce yourself to their colleague or associate, who might help you connect with them. Be friendly and genuine.

How Net with powerful executives

There's a common misconception that networking with powerful executives automatically confers power. However, true influence stems from mastering your role and excelling in it. While relationships can be beneficial, they only truly matter if you add value. Simply being visible isn't sufficient. Acting as a sycophant or a mere supporter may yield short-term gains in some scenarios, but it's a risky strategy that often results in losing respect from others and, more importantly, from yourself.

Instead, focus on authenticity and cultivate relationships across the organization. This approach not only contributes to your present but also establishes a lasting legacy. When engaging with others, aim not just to receive but also to give. Clearly communicate the value you bring and how it benefits them. Craft a compelling and memorable message. Sometimes, this may lead to obtaining a name and contact information for follow-up. It could be the initial step in building a connection. Occasionally, a senior executive might provide you with a valuable lead. Recognizing such opportunities is a positive sign, and it's up to you to navigate and progress further.

Get your job done.

A winsome personality is essential for success in all areas. You can't rely on functional expertise alone to grow. Even as a technical person, you will have to deal with clients, customers, and colleagues. So you need a range of skills, especially people skills, to be a well-rounded person. Otherwise, you will be stuck in your comfort zone and find it hard to advance and improve. Great managers are those who monitor the results while coaching their team to perform better. To be a coach, you need to be a smart, people-friendly leader.

Cultivating a CEO mindset

My exploration into effective leadership marked the initial phase of my journey towards adopting a CEO mindset. Understanding that leadership transcends mere authority, I recognized its essence in shouldering responsibility and making tough decisions for organizational improvement. A proficient leader listens actively to inputs while maintaining a clear vision, demonstrating adept communication, smart task delegation, and motivation to propel team members to excellence. These leadership qualities became integral to my personal growth.

Strategic thinking emerged as another pivotal characteristic that distinguishes a CEO. This involves scrutinizing current market trends, identifying opportunities, and formulating effective strategies to capitalize on them. Successful strategic thinking demands a forward-looking perspective, where CEOs envision the future of their companies and take calculated risks for sustained success. The capacity to anticipate and adapt to evolving business landscapes is imperative for navigating competitive markets. Enhancing my strategic thinking skills empowered me to outline the necessary steps for both personal and collective success.

Adaptability, too, proved indispensable for a CEO. In a dynamic world, the capability to adjust to new technologies, market dynamics, and customer demands is paramount. Embracing adaptability shifted my perception of change from a problem to an opportunity for growth and innovation. Resilience in challenging times necessitates a flexible mindset, a readiness to learn and unlearn, and the ability to pivot when circumstances demand. This attribute aided me in overcoming setbacks and emerging stronger and more determined.

While leadership, strategic thinking, and adaptability are fundamental, cultivating a CEO mindset requires perseverance as a driving force. The journey from a restricted mindset to a CEO mindset is fraught with obstacles, rejections, and failures. During adversity, perseverance becomes the catalyst propelling individuals towards their goals. I refused to let setbacks define me, viewing failure as a stepping stone towards success and utilizing it as a catalyst for learning, growth, and evolution. Through unwavering determination, I transcended limitations on my personal journey.

To fully embrace a CEO mindset, a commitment to lifelong learning is imperative. In a world in perpetual flux, a CEO is not defined by having all the answers but by a perpetual openness to learning, acquiring new skills, and seeking knowledge. This demands an insatiable curiosity, a quest for continuous improvement, and a willingness to step beyond one's comfort zone. Embracing lifelong learning allowed me to stay ahead of the curve, adapt to emerging technologies and trends, and make informed decisions for organizational betterment.

Therefore, cultivating a CEO mindset is not a one-time endeavor but a lifelong journey. It necessitates a blend of leadership, strategic thinking, adaptability, perseverance, and a commitment to perpetual learning. As individuals, we possess the agency to shape our destinies and contribute to building a better society. By adopting and refining these qualities, we can transform our limited mindsets into CEO mindsets, becoming catalysts for positive change in the world.

CHAPTER 6

Finish Unfinished Space

The art of decision-making plays a pivotal role in shaping our lives, influencing our choices, and steering us toward our goals. While this is a concept often studied academically, its true significance becomes apparent when applied to real-life scenarios. Our existence, indeed, is a reflection of the decisions we make. Here are key considerations to further refine and fortify your decision-making skills:

1. Consistent Practice
2. Learning from mistakes
3. Seeking Feedback
4. Knowledge Expansion and Diverse Perspectives

In the journey of life, decision-making is intertwined with critical junctures that may initially be beyond our control. From birth to adolescence, external influences guide our choices, laying the groundwork for independent decision-making in adulthood. However, the transition to adulthood requires a conscious shift towards self-awareness and autonomy.

In the teenage years, the decisions made—like what to wear or eat—may seem independent, yet they often carry the imprint of external influences or emotional states. As individuals mature into adulthood, their capacity to make decisions for themselves takes center stage. It is during this phase that true maturity manifests when decisions are made with heightened awareness, mindful of the long-term consequences.

While external factors may shape early life decisions, the ultimate responsibility rests on the individual to embrace self-awareness and steer their life's course. Developing this skill ensures that decisions are not merely influenced by external factors but are deliberate, purposeful choices aligned with personal values and goals.

Steps to Improve Decision-Making Skills:

1. Identify the issue: Recognize and comprehend the issue you are facing. Explain the problem, its significance, and what you aim to achieve by solving it.
2. Gather Information: Collect relevant data and facts to help examine the issue. Research the problem, consult experts, and use trustworthy sources of data.
3. Generate Alternatives: Create possible solutions or options for the issue. Brainstorm different ideas, be inventive, and consider the advantages and disadvantages of each option.
4. Evaluate Logically: Assess the options and choose the best one based on logic and reason. Use critical thinking, compare the options, and eliminate impractical or ineffective ones.
5. Assess the Impact: Evaluate the potential outcomes and consequences of your decision.

Consider short-term and long-term effects, risks and benefits, and the impact on yourself and others.

6. Implement the Decision: Execute your decision and take action. Plan the steps, carry out the plan, and monitor the results. Be adaptable and ready to adjust your decision if needed.
7. Decision-making skills are abilities that help you choose the best option among different alternatives. They involve using your intuition, reasoning, or a combination of both to analyze a situation and make a rational choice. Decision-making skills are important for various aspects of life, such as personal, professional, academic, and social. Examples of decision-making skills include:
8. Problem-solving: The ability to identify, understand, and solve a problem using logical steps and relevant information.
9. Leadership: the ability to motivate, inspire, and guide others towards a common goal or vision.
10. Reasoning: The ability to use facts, data, and evidence to support or reject a claim or argument.
11. Intuition: The ability to trust your gut feeling or instinct when faced with a decision or dilemma.
12. Teamwork: the ability to collaborate, communicate, and cooperate with others in a group or project.
13. Emotional intelligence is the ability to recognize, understand, and manage your own and others' emotions in different situations.

14. Creativity: the ability to generate new, original, and innovative ideas or solutions for a problem or challenge.

Build a good team.

A team transcends being merely a group of people working together; it embodies a family, a community, and a network built on support and trust. It is the synergy of diverse talents, skills, and personalities that harmoniously complement one another. A team is a shared vision, a common goal, and the embodiment of collective effort.

But how do you cultivate such a team? How do you create a cohesive, productive, and successful unit? Here are key tips to guide you:

Define Purpose and Objectives:

Clearly articulate why the team exists, what it aims to achieve, and how progress and performance will be measured. Ensuring everyone understands and aligns with these objectives provides a solid foundation for the team.

Select the right members:

Carefully curate your team with individuals possessing relevant expertise, experience, and enthusiasm for the mission. Seek diversity to inject creativity and innovation into the team dynamic.

Establish clear roles and responsibilities:

Assign tasks based on each team member's strengths, interests, and abilities. Clarify expectations and accountability for everyone, fostering a sense of purpose and direction.

Foster a Culture of Communication and Collaboration:

Encourage open and honest dialogue among team members. Create an environment where ideas, opinions, and feedback flow freely. Facilitate the exchange of information, resources, and best practices to support continuous learning and growth.

Celebrate Achievements and Challenges:

Recognize and appreciate each team member's contributions and efforts. Celebrate milestones and successes as a team. Embrace mistakes and failures as opportunities for learning. Keep the team motivated and inspired through a balanced acknowledgment of achievements and challenges.

By diligently following these tips, you can cultivate a high-performing team capable of achieving remarkable outcomes. Remember, building an effective team is not a distant aspiration; it is a tangible reality that you have the power to create.

Build good character

Before forming a solid team, it is necessary to develop good character. Building good character is the process of cultivating positive characteristics and ideals that drive your actions and decisions. Good character is essential for both personal and professional success, as well as societal contributions. Good character attributes include honesty, integrity, respect, responsibility, compassion, and courage.

To develop excellent character, you must practice these behaviors consistently and conscientiously. You must be honest with yourself and others, adhere to ethical values, respect yourself and others, accept responsibility for your actions and outcomes, demonstrate empathy and kindness, and face your fears and obstacles. You must also learn from your failures, seek criticism, and always strive to improve yourself.

By building good character, you can become a better person, a better leader, and a better citizen. Remember, good character is not something you are born with; it is something you create.

Switch the personality

Adapting one's character and behavior to various situations, akin to playing different roles in a movie, is the essence of personality switching. This skill proves invaluable in navigating the diverse challenges and opportunities presented by work, education, relationships, and hobbies. It is crucial to note that personality switching doesn't entail altering core values and beliefs, which are deeply rooted in factors such as culture, politics, environment, geography, childhood, experiences, and upbringing. These elements define one's true self, encompassing nature, habits, and behavior. Maintaining awareness and comfort with one's authentic self is paramount. Understanding when and how to switch personalities, as well as when to revert to one's true self, requires mindfulness. Personality switching is a learnable and practicable skill, yet it should never serve as a substitute for one's genuine identity.

In the realm of self-development, two indispensable factors are interpersonal skills and emotional intelligence.

Interpersonal skills encompass a range of abilities crucial for effective communication and interaction with others. These skills include:

- Listening: the capacity to attentively grasp and respond to what others are expressing.
- Empathy is the ability to understand and appreciate the feelings and perspectives of others.
- Assertiveness: expressing one's needs, opinions, and boundaries in a respectful and confident manner.
- Conflict resolution: navigating and resolving conflicts in a constructive and positive way.

Concurrently, emotional intelligence involves recognizing, comprehending, and managing both personal and others' emotions. It comprises skills like:

- Self-awareness: identifying and understanding one's emotions, strengths, weaknesses, and values.
- Self-regulation: controlling and adjusting emotions, impulses, and behaviors based on the situation and goals.
- Motivation: Utilizing emotions to drive oneself towards positive and meaningful actions.

- Social awareness: recognizing and understanding the emotions of others.
- Relationship management: nurturing and navigating relationships effectively.

Interpersonal skills and emotional intelligence are intertwined concepts pivotal for success in both personal and professional spheres. While interpersonal skills facilitate effective communication, emotional intelligence empowers individuals to recognize, understand, and manage emotions, fostering positive interactions and relationships.

Understand the clash between emotions.

First, understand your feelings. Emotions are strong forces that influence our ideas, behaviors, and overall well-being. However, emotions are not always predictable or sensible. Sometimes we have opposing or contradictory feelings, such as love and hatred, fear and exhilaration, or pleasure and despair. This might lead to an emotional battle or war, leaving us feeling confused, overwhelmed, or torn.

To deal with this circumstance, we must first grasp the nature and cause of our emotions, as well as their interaction with one another.

We also need to learn to use our emotions intelligently and productively, rather than reacting impulsively or adversely. We can do this by recognizing the opposite emotions that can balance or neutralize each other, such as happy and sad, confused and clear, or angry and calm. By using emotion against emotion, we can create harmony and peace within ourselves and become masters of our emotions.

Emotional intelligence is a multifaceted skill set that encompasses the effective management of one's emotions and adept interaction with others. It comprises various intelligences, including:

- Intra-personal intelligence is the capacity to understand oneself and one's emotions, fostering self-awareness and emotional insight.
- Visual intelligence is the ability to create mental images and visualize concepts, contributing to creative thinking and problem-solving.
- Logical Intelligence: Proficiency in reasoning and problem-solving using numerical and logical frameworks, aiding in analytical decision-making.
- Kinesthetic intelligence is the skill of expressing oneself physically and understanding the body's movements, promoting effective communication through non-verbal cues.
- Music intelligence is the ability to appreciate, create, and comprehend sounds, rhythms, and musical patterns, contributing to a heightened sensitivity to auditory stimuli.

To enhance emotional intelligence, it is valuable to develop proficiency in these different intelligences. By nurturing self-awareness, honing visual and logical thinking, refining kinesthetic expression, and appreciating the nuances of music, individuals can enrich their overall emotional intelligence. This holistic approach to emotional intelligence not only strengthens personal well-being but also fosters meaningful connections and relationships with others.

Is this conversation helpful so far?

Emotional trauma

First, understand your feelings. Emotions are strong forces that influence our ideas, behaviors, and overall well-being. However, emotions are not always predictable or sensible. Sometimes we have opposing or contradictory feelings, such as love and hatred, fear and exhilaration, or pleasure and despair. This might lead to an emotional battle or war, leaving us feeling confused, overwhelmed, or torn.

To deal with this circumstance, we must first grasp the nature and cause of our emotions, as well as their interaction with one another.

We also need to learn to use our emotions intelligently and productively, rather than reacting impulsively or adversely.

Practice positive attitude

A positive attitude is a method of thinking that helps you see the good in everything. It enables you to overcome obstacles, deal with stress, and achieve your objectives. A cheerful attitude increases your happiness, health, and attractiveness to others. To maintain a cheerful mindset, you must cultivate thankfulness, optimism, and compassion. Focus on your strengths, not your faults. You should learn from your errors, not linger on them. You should surround yourself with positive individuals, not negative ones. A happy attitude is a decision you can make every day.

Practice silent

Practicing silence is the habit of being quiet and mindful in different situations. It is not about avoiding communication or expression but about choosing when and how to speak or act. Practicing silence can help you build a strong personality in many ways, such as:

- improving your focus and concentration. By being silent, you can pay more attention to your thoughts, feelings, and surroundings. You can also avoid distractions and interruptions that can affect your productivity and creativity.
- enhancing your listening and understanding. By being silent, you can listen more actively and empathetically to others. You can also understand yourself better and discover your inner wisdom and values.
- developing your confidence and respect. By being silent, you can show respect and appreciation for others and their opinions. You can also gain respect and trust from others who value your silence and your words.
- Practicing silence is an attitude that can make you a better person and a better leader.

Gratitude

Attitude without appreciation is meaningless. When it comes to thankfulness, I'd want to show my appreciation here as well, because all I've learned and gained today is due to the blessings of my parents, grandparents, elders, ancestors, teachers, mentors, relatives, and friends. As an Indian, I would like to thank my motherland, my nation, first. Gratitude is the feeling of appreciation and thankfulness for the people, things, and experiences that enrich our lives. Gratitude is not only a positive emotion but also a powerful attitude that can transform our outlook and well-being. Gratitude can help us:

- Recognize and value what we have, rather than focusing on what we lack or want.
- express our gratitude to others and strengthen our relationships and connections.
- Attract more goodness and abundance into our lives by being open and receptive to the opportunities and blessings that come our way.

Practice spirituality.

When it comes to inner self-development, let me share my own experience with spirituality. Spirituality is the only way to realize your full potential and gain self-awareness. This is still something I'm learning, but it's already helping me in a lot of ways. And, to be clear, spirituality is not the same as religion, as each religion has its own unique method of practicing spirituality. There are several ways to practice it. My grandparents practiced spirituality, and I grew up watching them do so. My father also suggested certain books to help me grasp spirituality. When I arrived in Ahmedabad, I met others who also practiced it. At first, I visited the ISKCON temple in Ahmedabad, where I learned a lot about spirituality and yoga. Yoga is one of the ways to practice spirituality, and in Indian culture, there are many types of yoga.

In Ahmedabad, during my drama classes, I met Utsavi, Bharat, and Mansi, from whom I learned Om chanting and the extreme healing process through spirituality. Therefore, as a corporate employee, when I needed healing, it all helped me a lot. So practice spirituality to unlock your true self-realization, no matter which path you choose.

Think outside the box

Thinking outside the box is the ability to generate new, original, and creative ideas or solutions that go beyond the conventional or expected. Thinking outside the box can help you:

- overcome challenges and problems that seem impossible or difficult to solve.
- Discover new opportunities and possibilities that others may overlook or ignore.
- Innovate and create new products, services, or processes that can benefit yourself and others.
- Learn and grow as a person, a professional, and a leader.

To think outside the box, you need to:

- Challenge your assumptions and beliefs, and question the status quo and the norms.
- Explore different perspectives and viewpoints, and seek inspiration from diverse sources and experiences.

- Experiment and try new things, and learn from your failures and feedback.
- Have an open and curious mind and a positive and optimistic attitude.
- I'm not telling you to follow my suggestion or believe everything you have been taught, but I suggest you make your own way of learning.

CHAPTER 7

Balance the Unbalanced

Life is full of unbalance. One faces challenges, changes, and uncertainties every day. One has to juggle multiple roles, responsibilities, and expectations. One has to deal with stress, pressure, and competition. The answer is to balance the imbalance. To balance the unbalance means to accept the reality of life, to embrace the diversity of experiences, and to adapt to the situations. It means to seek harmony within oneself, with others, and with the environment. It means to find the right equilibrium between work and play, between action and rest, and between giving and receiving. To balance the imbalance is to live a fulfilling and meaningful life.

I have learned that there are four types of zones that we live in:

- Comfort zone
- Fear zone
- Learning zone
- Growth zone

In the past few years, a profound realization has dawned on me. I've observed that many individuals tend to navigate through life within the confines of either the comfort zone or the fear zone. However, those who dare to venture beyond and step into the learning zone often unlock a pathway to substantial personal growth. While

I may not be an expert on the subject of growth, as I find myself still immersed in the continuous journey of learning, I've gained valuable insights from my experiences with comfort and fear.

Having spent time in a slum area, I've witnessed that a significant portion of the population resides firmly within the fear zone. Strikingly, this phenomenon is not exclusive to economically disadvantaged areas, as many individuals from the middle class also find themselves ensnared in the clutches of the fear zone. Characterized by low self-confidence, a propensity for making excuses, and a vulnerability to the opinions of others, the fear zone can be a stifling space.

Individuals' motivation

Introversion initially defined my personality, but a transformative switch occurred when I began to take note of the significance of collaborating with employees who truly make a difference. Beyond the confines of job titles, some individuals wield a remarkable impact that surpasses their official positions. The key lies not only in focusing on those at the apex of the organizational hierarchy but also in recognizing the wide-reaching influence of individuals at the foundational level.

A prime example lies in those often-underestimated figures, such as the 'assistants' to powerful leaders, who operate as silent influencers behind the scenes. In my own journey, I vividly recall the invaluable support provided by Lakhan Bhai. Despite his seemingly unassuming role, he played a pivotal role by sharing pertinent books related to my field, providing additional valuable resources and information, and even opening doors to potential career opportunities abroad. These quiet influencers, often working in the shadows, act as indispensable facilitators in the business realm, yet their contributions frequently remain overshadowed by more prominent departments.

Dependency

Dependency, fundamentally defined as the need for or influence exerted by someone or something else, encompasses diverse meanings and effects contingent on various situations and perspectives. My realization of this truth came belatedly, but it became apparent that navigating through different life scenarios, whether in corporate or social realms, often necessitates some form of dependency. Invariably, we all find ourselves reliant on certain elements, which, if unchecked, can transform into limiting factors.

A personal illustration of this surfaced when I decided to step out of my comfort zone, encountering an unexpected challenge: food. This predicament is a shared experience for many individuals who have resided in hostels. Yet, dependency extends beyond mere dietary needs. In the slums, alcohol addiction serves as another poignant example. Fortunately, being from Gujarat, a dry state in India, I was spared this particular dependency. It underscores the point that dependency can manifest in myriad forms, be it reliance on substances or individuals that hinder personal progress.

In the corporate landscape, distinct types of dependency emerge:

1. Economic Dependency: This occurs when a country or region leans on another for trade, aid,

or resources, potentially affecting the development, growth, and autonomy of the dependent party.

2. Psychological dependency: This materializes when an individual finds emotional support, comfort, or pleasure in another person or substance, impacting mental health, well-being, and personal freedom.
3. Technological Dependency: This manifests when an individual or society heavily relies on technology for communication, education, entertainment, or work. This reliance can influence the skills, creativity, and social interactions of the dependent entity.

The dichotomy of dependency lies in its potential to be both constructive and detrimental, contingent on the degree, nature, and outcomes of that dependency. To effectively manage dependency, one must discern the merits and drawbacks, striking a delicate balance between dependency and self-reliance. Recognizing when and where dependency adds value while simultaneously cultivating the ability to stand independently is crucial for achieving harmonious equilibrium in personal and professional spheres.

Money management

Finance is essential for both corporate and personal success. However, many of us ignore financial management in our personal lives. I understood this when I entered the corporate world. I learned how important it is to manage money well. If you want to improve your financial management skills, you can read many books on this topic. I am also reading about it and learning more about it. I realized that most of the things I bought were not worth it. Budgeting is important. Money management is the process of tracking and planning how to use money. For corporations, money management involves raising and using money, budgeting, spending, saving, and investing. A firm's budgeting depends on its business strategies. Money management helps corporations cut down on unnecessary expenses, increase cash flow, and reach their financial goals. I learned some solutions, like:

Financial management software: These are tools that help to automate and simplify financial transactions and management. When I came to Ahmedabad, Saurabh bhai suggested I install an app on my mobile that helped us split our expenses equally. You might already know about it if you live in a PG or a hostel.

Portfolio management and investment management: These are methods of managing and making investment decisions for groups of funds. They aim to increase returns and decrease risks for investors.

Financial advisors and consultants: These are professionals who provide money management services and advice to corporate clients. This is the topic I am still learning about.

Time management

Time management is a skill that helps us balance our lives. I realized that time has value and that everyone's time is valuable. No one will give you attention here because everyone is busy with their work. Most of us realize the importance of time. When I was in college, I was so lazy. I had a bad habit of sleeping late. It became more serious because I was sleeping more than 12 hours a day. My father asked me if I wanted to visit a doctor. I said, Why? He said you were sleeping a lot. I didn't understand then because I thought sleeping and the doctor had no connection. Later, I realized that sleeping a lot could be a cause or symptom of unstable mental health or depression. Well, my mother's taunts were stronger than that. But when it comes to time management, many problems can be solved, like,

Reducing stress and anxiety

Increasing productivity and efficiency

Improving performance and quality

Enhancing creativity and innovation

Balancing work and life,

Some strategies for time management are:

Specific, Measurable, Achievable, Relevant, and Time-bound

Planning ahead and creating a daily or weekly schedule

Breaking down large or complex tasks into smaller and simpler ones

Using tools and apps to track and manage your time

Eliminating or minimizing distractions and interruptions

Never let die your hobbies.

I have a deep reason for writing about this topic. When I entered the corporate world, I noticed that people used to include hobbies in their resumes or CVs. But over time, this heading 'hobbies' vanished from their resume and their lives. This is not only true for corporate employees, but for every working professional in India. Living a robotic life is not worthwhile, right? I also observed that once you have more experience in your resume, HR does not pay attention to this heading.

Hobbies are activities that we do for fun, pleasure, and personal growth. They are not related to our work or obligations but rather to our passions and interests. Hobbies can help us relieve stress, express ourselves, learn new skills, meet new people, and enjoy life. However, many of us tend to neglect our hobbies as we get busy with our work and responsibilities. We may think that hobbies are not important or that we do not have time for them. We may also lose interest or motivation in our hobbies over time. This is unfortunate, because hobbies can make us happier, healthier, and more fulfilled. That is why we should never let our hobbies die. We should always find time and ways to pursue our hobbies, no matter how old or busy we are. We should also try to explore new hobbies or revive old ones that we have forgotten. Hobbies can keep us alive and excited and remind us of who we are and what we love.

This topic is very important to me because I had many hobbies before joining the corporate world. I enjoyed playing chess, guitar, and flute, singing, skating, reading, and writing. I had so many hobbies because I liked to spend time with myself as an introvert. But after getting a corporate job, I did not have enough time for all my hobbies.

Magic of words

Words can create or destroy, heal or hurt, inspire or discourage. Words can shape our reality and influence our emotions. Words can also affect how others perceive us and how we perceive ourselves. That is why we should be careful and mindful of the words we use. We should choose words that are positive, accurate, respectful, and meaningful. We should avoid words that are negative, vague, rude, or meaningless. By choosing our words wisely. Our mindset is largely influenced by our subconscious mind, which controls our beliefs, habits, skills, and talents. Words are powerful because our subconscious mind does not distinguish between positive and negative. Whatever we say, see, or hear, our subconscious mind acts on it. If we strongly believe in something, our subconscious mind works to make it happen. This affects our body and our reality. Some books suggest that words are powerful tools for affirmations and manifestation. Sometimes, we say too much in anger and later regret it. But controlling our senses is important. This is the beginning of spirituality. If we learn this, our focus level will increase automatically.

Never let your inner child die.

In a professional setting, the importance of incorporating humor often gets overshadowed by the demands of work, leading to heightened anxiety and stress. It is crucial to maintain a connection with the core values of life while navigating the challenges of the professional realm.

Our inner child embodies the playful, curious, and adventurous facets of our being. It symbolizes the part of us that thrives on exploration, learning, and enjoyment—a genuine expression of our emotions. Over time, however, the demands of adulthood may cause us to lose touch with this inner child. The pressures of work and responsibilities, coupled with societal expectations, compel us to adopt a more mature façade, often stifling our ability to live and relish life to the fullest.

Observing elderly individuals revert to childlike joy in their later years serves as a poignant reminder. This regression is not an anomaly but a testament to the yearning for the unbridled living experienced in childhood. Many adults, engrossed in the pursuit of material possessions, societal approval, and financial success, find themselves longing for the carefree moments of their youth during retirement.

Childhood, being the purest form of living and expressing, is a time when individuals live in the moment. To truly live, it is imperative to prevent the demise of our inner child. Embracing the simplicity and joy found in life's small pleasures keeps this inner child alive. In certain situations, it becomes essential to temporarily set aside the weight of intellect and act with the unbridled enthusiasm characteristic of a child. It's noteworthy that some of the most intelligent individuals often exhibit childlike qualities, proving that balancing seriousness with the lighthearted spirit of an inner child can lead to a more fulfilling and well-rounded life.

CHAPTER 8

To do list

I am eager to enhance my understanding and cultivate a CEO mindset to propel me toward achieving both personal and professional aspirations while positively impacting the world. I acknowledge that possessing a CEO mindset extends beyond merely holding a position of authority; it encompasses having a well-defined vision, a strategic plan, and the ability to execute it effectively. This mindset involves embracing resilience, fostering innovation, and embodying an entrepreneurial spirit. Additionally, it requires leadership characterized by transparency, integrity, and empathy.

Recognizing the challenges in developing a CEO mindset, I am committed to continual learning, regular practice, and actively seeking feedback. Overcoming fears, doubts, and obstacles is an inherent part of this journey. To facilitate my growth, I have outlined a to-do list that serves as a roadmap for acquiring the necessary skills and mastering the mindset of a CEO.

Here is my list:

1. HR and transparency: I want to learn how to attract, retain, and develop the best talent for any organization. I also want to learn how to communicate effectively and honestly with the team, stakeholders, and customers. I want to learn

how to create a culture of trust, collaboration, and accountability.

2. Project management: I want to learn how to plan, execute, and control projects successfully. I want to learn how to manage time, resources, and risks. I want to learn how to deliver quality results on time and on budget.
3. Resilience: I want to learn how to cope with stress, uncertainty, and failure. I want to learn how to bounce back from setbacks and challenges. I want to learn how to grow from feedback and criticism.
4. Entrepreneurial mindset: I want to learn how to think creatively and innovatively. I want to learn how to identify and seize opportunities. I want to learn how to take calculated risks and experiment with new ideas.
5. Innovation and technologies: I want to learn how to use data, innovation, and technologies to create value and solve problems. I want to learn how to leverage the latest tools and trends to optimize and improve processes, products, and services.
6. Strategies and development: I want to learn how to formulate, implement, and evaluate strategies for success. I want to learn how to use various analytical tools and frameworks to make informed decisions. I want to learn how to develop myself and my organization for long-term growth.

Edit your circle

The adage "Better alone than in bad company" underscores the significance of choosing our associates wisely, emphasizing the impact of our social circles on our lives. Similarly, the proverb "You are what you consume the most" accentuates how our habits and choices mold our character and shape our destiny. Personal experiences have affirmed the validity of these proverbs in my life.

In a previous chapter, I recounted my journey of seeking purpose by joining a communist group. However, preceding this, I found myself involved with a street gang, driven by the desire to channel my influence toward a cause. Prior to that phase, my innocence and obedience prevailed, reflecting the influence of my friends at the time. As I navigated through life, my attraction toward the powerful stemmed from the realization that the world was governed by such individuals. Yet, this trajectory failed to yield any meaningful outcomes.

The key takeaway is that achieving one's goals may not necessarily require a change in location but often demands a shift in one's circle. Evaluating the influences in our lives becomes crucial—either transforming negative influences into positive ones or severing ties altogether. Continuous self-monitoring is imperative to ensure that we do not inadvertently become purveyors of negativity for others.

Live Like an Artist

Are you yearning to infuse vibrancy into your professional life? Do you aspire to unlock heightened levels of creativity, productivity, and overall happiness? The key might be found in adopting the mindset of an artist in your workplace—an approach characterized by living for, with, and through art.

Living for art entails cultivating a profound passion, vision, and mission in your work. It means conquering challenges, leaving an indelible mark on others, and embodying the spirit of pioneers in your field. Picture individuals like my music teacher, Gaurav Kapadiya, who unearths the beauty of music in a town where it's often dismissed as mere noise. Consider my drama teacher, Prashant Jadav, who preserves the essence of drama in a world that sometimes reduces it to mere acting. These individuals live for art in their work, and their impact is nothing short of remarkable.

Living with art involves immersing yourself in a world of creativity, appreciation, and continual learning. It means developing a refined taste, nurturing curiosity, and embracing diversity in your endeavors. I draw inspiration from my own experiences, where friends and influencers from the realm of art have played a pivotal role. Since joining Instagram in 2017, I've discovered an entire universe of artistic expression. Engaging with various artists and content creators has been an enlightening experience, enriching my perspective and contributing to my personal and professional growth. I am actively living with art at work, and the profound enjoyment it brings is undeniable.

Humour

Humor is the ability to make others laugh or to laugh at yourself. It is a valuable skill that can improve your work and personal life in many ways. But humor is not something that I was born with or that I learned easily. It is something that I had to develop and that I still struggle with. I am an introverted person. I avoid talking too much, socializing, and being in the spotlight.

I prefer to be alone, with a few close friends, or in the background. I find it hard to connect with and understand people, especially those who are different from me, but humor is not my forte. I was not good at making jokes, telling stories, or being witty. I was not good at laughing at myself, at life, or at anything. I was too serious, too shy, and too sensitive.

During my teenage years, I grappled with a surge of emotions that often manifested as anger. I found it challenging to accept criticism, deal with conflicts, or navigate my own emotional responses. Any mention of my mistakes or encounters with irritation or anger from others triggered strong reactions within me. In those moments, I felt a profound sense of being wronged, offended, or hurt.

Regrettably, my coping mechanisms at the time were far from constructive. Faced with criticism, irritation, or anger, I would impulsively lash out, withdraw into silence, or choose to escape physically or emotionally. This reactionary behavior stemmed from a lack of understanding about how to effectively manage criticism, handle conflicts, and process my own emotions.

I realized that humor could help me with that. It could help me accept my flaws, cope with stress, and deal with difficulties. It could help me see things from a different perspective, find the silver lining, and learn the lesson. It could help me be more confident, resilient, and optimistic.

Editing my mistake

We all make mistakes in life. Some are small, some are big, some are trivial, and some are crucial. But what matters is not how many mistakes we make, but how we learn from them and grow.

Consistency

Consistency stands as the cornerstone of success across various domains, be it content creation, competitive exams, music, acting, or chess. The key lies in maintaining a steadfast approach to your efforts and outputs. Establishing a clear goal, a meticulous plan, and a well-structured schedule is crucial. Despite its paramount importance, I, personally, grappled with consistency throughout my life, often initiating endeavors but faltering in completing them. Challenges such as a lack of resources, time constraints, or waning motivation contributed to my struggles. I came to understand that the absence of applause or recognition can make consistency particularly challenging.

To rectify this, I started setting realistic goals, crafting detailed yet flexible plans, and adhering to a regular and rewarding schedule. Additionally, finding intrinsic motivation, tracking progress, and celebrating achievements became essential practices. Seeking guidance, feedback, and support from others and cultivating accountability, adaptability, and resilience were also crucial steps in overcoming this challenge.

Laziness

Laziness, the nemesis of productivity and happiness, manifests as the tendency to avoid, delay, or perform tasks half-heartedly. I found myself succumbing to laziness, often neglecting my health, relationships, and responsibilities. At one point, excessive sleep raised concerns, leading to the realization that laziness isn't merely a choice but can be symptomatic of deeper issues, such as depression.

Overcoming this mistake required a thorough examination of the root causes of laziness, including stress, fear, boredom, or a lack of purpose. Establishing a healthy and balanced routine, incorporating physical activity, mental stimulation, social interaction, and personal growth, became essential. Positive and negative reinforcement strategies were employed to motivate myself while consciously avoiding distractions like TV, phone, or the internet that contributed to laziness.

Never Completing Started Projects

Completing initiated projects signifies commitment, completion, and professionalism. Unfortunately, I had a habit of leaving things incomplete, facing challenges, losing interest, or changing my focus. I would start writing books, songs, or scripts, but struggled with discipline and perseverance.

The remedy involved breaking down projects into manageable tasks, setting deadlines and milestones, and tracking progress. Shifting my focus to the benefits and outcomes of completion, seeking feedback and encouragement from others, and overcoming fears and doubts were integral to overcoming this mistake.

Lack of focus and patience

Focusing on one thing at a time and exercising patience are skills synonymous with concentration and persistence. Despite my curiosity and ambition, I found myself multitasking, switching interests, and lacking patience. I studied multiple subjects, tried various careers, and pursued numerous goals, but struggled to master or achieve anything.

To address this, I started prioritizing and selecting one meaningful goal, career, or subject at a time, devoting my energy and attention to it. Additionally, practicing concentration and persistence through exercises, meditations, and challenges became pivotal. Cultivating gratitude, respect, and acceptance further helped in appreciating the journey rather than fixating on immediate results.

Trusting too quickly

Trust forms the bedrock of any relationship, requiring belief in the honesty and reliability of others. Unfortunately, I had a tendency to trust too quickly, often leading to situations where trust was taken advantage of.

The lesson learned involves being cautious and aware, ensuring that trust is earned rather than freely given. It's essential not to take anyone for granted and to remain vigilant in assessing the honesty and integrity of those we place our trust in.

Never be influenced too much by social media.

Social media platforms offer both utility and entertainment, yet their impact can be double-edged, ranging from beneficial to detrimental. They possess the potential to influence our mood, behavior, and decisions, sometimes steering us in unfavorable directions. These platforms expose us to a myriad of information, not all of which is accurate or impartial, thereby manipulating our emotions, shaping our opinions, and even influencing our actions. Moreover, constant exposure to curated versions of others' lives can lead to detrimental comparisons, fostering feelings of insecurity, discontentment, or unhappiness.

To navigate the complexities of social media responsibly, it is imperative to adopt an informed, critical, and discerning approach. Developing this approach involves being cognizant of the sources, motives, and potential effects of the information we encounter. A critical mindset is crucial for evaluating the accuracy, reliability, and validity of the content we consume, allowing us to differentiate between credible information and misinformation.

Furthermore, being selective about the platforms, accounts, and content we engage with is essential. Setting boundaries and consciously managing the time we spend on these platforms helps mitigate the negative impact they can have on our mental well-being.

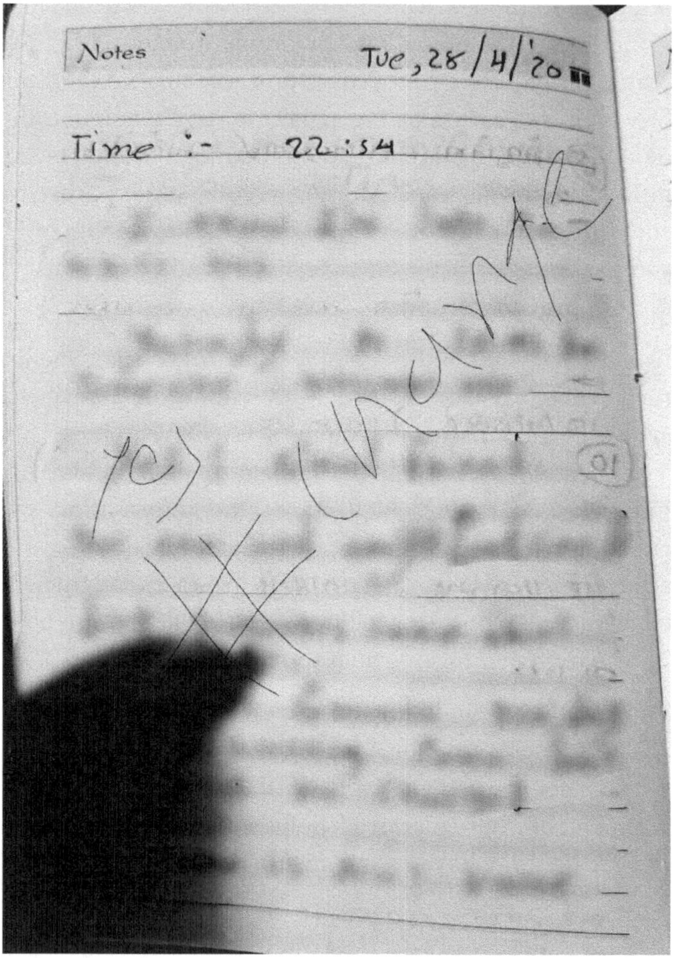
Notes
Tue, 28/4/'20
Time :- 22:54
10
Change

Conclusion

My main message in this book is that you can achieve anything you want if you have the right mindset, attitude, and action. You can change your life and the lives of others for the better. You can be a leader, a creator, and a learner. You can be a CEO, or whatever you aspire to be.

This book has changed my life and perspective in many ways. It has helped me reflect on my journey, express my thoughts and feelings, and share my wisdom and experience. It has also helped me connect with you, my readers, and with my 'kuchikus', my true strength, my audience. It has also helped me fulfill one of my goals, which was to write my own story.

I hope this book has also changed your life and perspective in some ways. I hope it has inspired you, motivated you, and empowered you. I hope it has given you some insights, tips, and tools. I hope it has made you laugh, cry, and think.

Now, I want to invite you to take action. Don't just read this book, but apply what you have learned. Don't just listen to my story; write your own story. Don't just follow my advice, but find your own voice. Don't just dream, but do.

I believe in you, and I support you. You have the potential, the power, and the passion. You have the mindset, the attitude, and the action. You have the slum, the CEO, and everything in between.

You have everything you need to succeed. Go for it.

Behind the Scenes

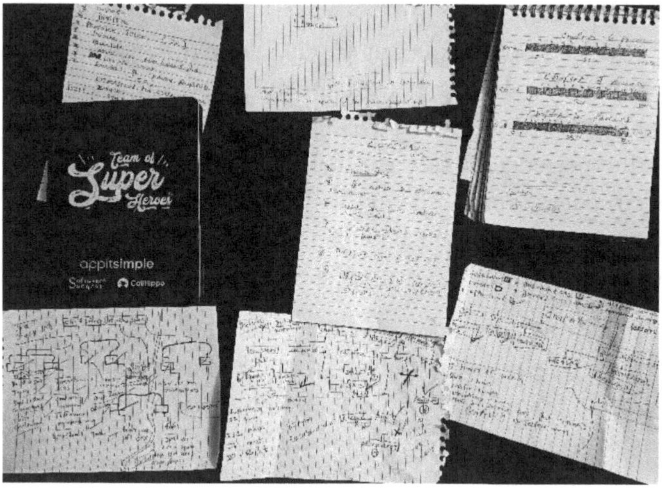

Purpose of Writing this Book

Why did I write this book? What was my motivation, intention, and goal? Who was my target audience, and what did they need and benefit from this book? How do I thank and acknowledge my readers, supporters, and sources? These are the questions that I have right now, but honestly, I didn't decide them before because it was my first book.

I wrote this book because I wanted to share my story and my learning with the world. I don't know if it will inspire you or not or influence you or not. I wanted to contribute, create, and communicate something valuable and meaningful. I wanted to fulfill one of my goals, which was to write my own story that reflects ground-level experiences where mindset is important.

My motivation for writing this book came from my own experience and observation. I saw that many people, especially in slums and small towns, faced similar problems and challenges as I did. I also saw that many people had similar goals and visions to mine. I wanted to help them and myself overcome the problems and challenges and achieve the goals and visions.

My goal for writing this book was to connect with others who were interested in developing my mindset and my learning. I wanted to build a network and a team of like-minded people who could support, encourage, and collaborate with each other. I wanted to create a community and a culture of learning, creating, and leading.

Behind the Scenes

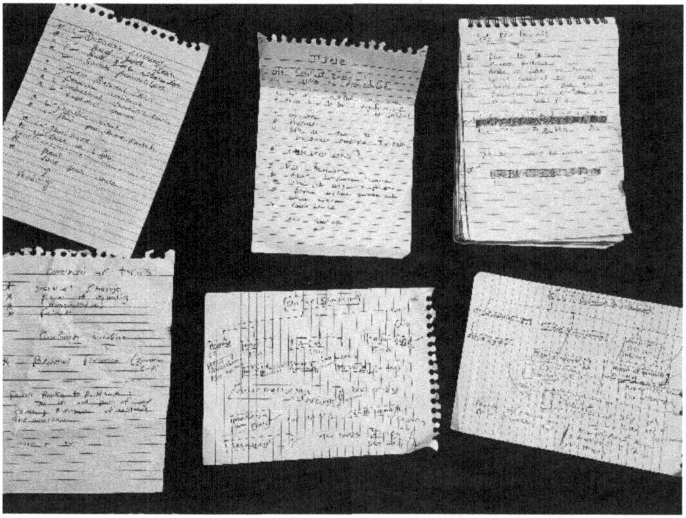

I seriously don't know my target audience for this book. But anyone who wanted to change their life and the lives of others for the better. It could be book lovers, students, leaders, or my inspirations. It could be anyone who wanted to learn, create, and lead. It could be anyone who wanted to develop their mindset from slum to CEO, or whatever they aspired to be.

I want to thank and acknowledge my readers for their time, attention, and feedback. I appreciate your interest, curiosity, and engagement. I value your opinions, questions, and suggestions. I respect your perspectives, experiences, and stories. I love your support, encouragement, and collaboration.

I want to especially thank my mother, Manju ben Laljibhai Solanki, and my father, Lajibhai Govindbhai Solanki, for giving me life and raising me with love and values. I want to also thank my late grandparents, my family members, and my sisters and brothers for being there for me and supporting me. I also want to thank my teachers and mentors. I also want to thank my cousins, Rahul and his godfather, Saishav Shah, and my supporters, Arpit Shah and Pankil Bhai, for helping me and encouraging me. I want to also thank my true potential, my friends, who are too many to name; some of them are online as well as long-distance.